THE **MINI** ROUGH GUIDE TO
LISBON

YOUR TAILOR-MADE TRIP
STARTS HERE

Tailor-made trips and unique adventures crafted by local experts

Rough Guides has been inspiring travellers for more than 35 years. Leave it to our local experts to create your perfect itinerary and book it at local rates.

Don't follow the crowd – find your own path.

HOW ROUGHGUIDES.COM/TRIPS WORKS

STEP 1 Pick your dream destination, tell us what you want and submit an enquiry.

STEP 2 Fill in a short form to tell your local expert about your dream trip and preferences.

STEP 3 Our local expert will craft your tailor-made itinerary. You'll be able to tweak and refine it until you're completely satisfied.

STEP 4 Book online with ease, pack your bags and enjoy the trip! Our local expert will be on hand 24/7 while you're on the road.

PLAN AND BOOK YOUR TRIP AT
ROUGHGUIDES.COM/TRIPS

HOW TO DOWNLOAD YOUR FREE EBOOK

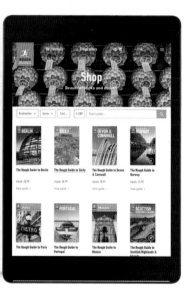

1. Visit **www.roughguides. com/free-ebook** or scan the **QR code** below

2. Enter the code **lisbon394**

3. Follow the simple step-by-step instructions

For troubleshooting contact: mail@roughguides.com

10 THINGS NOT TO MISS

A PERFECT DAY

9.00am

Start the day. Tuck into a breakfast of coffee and pastries at a laid-back café in Alfama, Lisbon's steeply inclined, characterful Moorish district that is topped by the Castelo de São Jorge. Then slowly saunter around the corner to Lisbon's cathedral. The Sé is a handsome, defensive-looking place of worship dating from the 12th century, and forms a contrast to the web of narrow Alfama lanes.

11.00am

Castle views. From here it's a picturesque meander through alleys splashed with vibrantly colourful *azulejos* (tiles), up the steep incline to the Castelo de São Jorge, with sweeping panoramic views over the city and the River Tagus.

1.00pm

Lunch. Time for a lazy lunch of grilled sardines or *bacalhau* (salted cod). In one of the family-run restaurants in the backstreets of Alfama.

2.30pm

Tram ride. Take a trip on Lisbon's most picturesque tram ride, No. 28, and head down to the Baixa district, an appealing grid of old-fashioned streets. Have a wander around the Praça do Comércio, whose proud colonnades overlook the Tagus, before taking a bus westwards along the waterfront to Belém, Lisbon's monumental district.

3.30pm

Belém. Visit the fantastical Mosteiro dos Jerónimos, a frenzy of elaborate carving that's somehow otherworldly in

IN **LISBON**

its magnificence, and the Torre de Belém, nearby, Lisbon's classic landmark.

5.00pm

Custard tarts. Follow these historic sights in Belém with one of Lisbon's finest *pastéis* (custard tarts) (see page 110), which sells well over 10,000 *pastéis* a day, is just the place to sample these delicious, warm-from-the-oven confections of delight. Head back to your hotel to relax and perhaps have an *aperitivo* before heading out again for dinner in Alfama.

8.00pm

Dinner in Alfama. Dine at Chapitô á Mesa in Alfama (see page 106), perched just below Castelo de São Jorge. The dining room is wrapped by windows on all sides and the lights of the city sparkle below. It's a fantastic way to top off a perfect day in Lisbon.

10.00pm

Fado experience. To experience traditional Portuguese soul music, try a tiny, out-of-the-way place nearby in Alfama, where locals are not averse to giving their all in rendering Portugal's songs of life and loss.

11.30pm

On the town. By this time the bar scene at Bairro Alto is just getting going. If you are ready to party, head back into town to see the bar-lined streets take on a carnival, street party vibe. Bar hop until you drop, or head off to Lux (see page 88), Lisbon's finest club, on the waterfront. You can party on from here and watch the dawn of a new day from the terrace.

CONTENTS

OVERVIEW

Lying with its back to Spain and its face to the Atlantic Ocean, Europe's most westerly country is about three-quarters the size of England. Around 3 million of its 10.3 million inhabitants live in Lisbon, the capital, which sits halfway down the coast on the estuary of the River Tagus (Tejo in Portuguese). The city is built over a number of hills on the right bank, facing south, at the estuary's narrowest point, where it shrinks to around 3km (2 miles). Europe's second longest bridge reaches across the estuary to the expansive delta on the far side.

LAID-BACK CAPITAL

Lisbon's great days are over, its colonies gone. Fortunes have risen and fallen dramatically over the course of its 3,000-year history. Even in recent times, a burst of economic activity that was sparked by the EU at the end of the 20th century is a distant memory, as Portugal struggled to overcome the fallout of the 2008 crisis and the subsequent austerity measures under the EU bailout. After 2014, the country saw a steady recovery until, like all European countries, the pandemic in 2020 took its toll.

Lisbon may have corners that are cutting edge, in its nightlife, designer boutiques and galleries and chic restaurants, but it is also a place that resonates with the difficult-to-define Portuguese characteristic of *saudade* (nostalgia), enjoying a slightly regretful, drawn-out retirement from its time as centre of empire and greatness.

A global language

There are 260 million Portuguese speakers in the world, making it the sixth most-spoken language in the world.

A tram ride through steep, narrow streets

Even when tourists began to arrive in any number, in the 20th century, Lisbon was seen as a lovely but laid-back provincial capital, known more for the charms of the narrow Moorish-style streets, the beauty of its hand-painted ceramic tiles and occasional ornate architectural flourishes than for economic dynamism. With its neighbourhoods clustered on the sides of hills along the placid Tagus, there are gentle reminders everywhere of Lisbon's distant past: the Phoenician profile of the modern fishing boats; the Moorish expertise with painted tiles; the pained notes of *fado*'s longing and lament.

STREETS AND VIEWPOINTS

The narrow whitewashed streets of the old Moorish neighbourhood, Alfama, twist and turn; they remain the heart of a modest, working-class, inner-city village. Here and elsewhere, *Lisboetas* decorate their balconies with flowerpots, their walls with colourful tiles, and the pavements with mosaics. Building and restoration work is everywhere in evidence, but it is a slow and expensive business and there is a lot to do.

Local women carry bags of bread and groceries up and down Lisbon's hills without complaint, but visitors may prefer to opt for one of the charming century-old electric trams that still trundle through the city, or let one of the eccentric yellow funiculars take the strain. Wandering is rewarded with picturesque nooks or brilliant panoramic views of the city's red-tiled rooftops stepped down towards the river. Whether from one of the lookouts in Alfama, the gardens of Castelo de São Jorge (St George's Castle) or the top of Santa Justa, the iron lift that used to transport workers and residents from the Baixa (lower) to the Bairro Alto (upper neighbourhood), *Lisboetas* never miss an opportunity to take in the whole of their city in its sun-kissed splendour.

Although the cold Atlantic lies only a few kilometres downriver, Lisbon feels decidedly Mediterranean. A sheltered, south-facing location and mild winters allow palm trees and bird-of-paradise flowers to flourish, and the balmy weather encourages an unhurried pace.

Despite the inescapable presence of a greater past, this is a modern, cosmopolitan capital, which has a sense of the world outside. The city's streets teem with people of diverse ethnicity and dress. Many are immigrants from Portugal's former African colonies – Angola, Cape Verde, Mozambique – or from Brazil, Macau and Goa, who arrived in Lisbon and soon founded their own little colonies, speaking a slightly softer version of the language and adding spice to the cuisine.

LISBOA CARD

Lisbon's tourist offices offer a discount Lisboa Card that entitles holders to free Metro (subway), bus, tram and lift transport; free entry into 35 museums and monuments; plus discounts of up to 50 percent in other places of interest, as well as some shops and tours. The card (available for one, two or three days) covers nearly everything of interest to visitors, including sights outside Lisbon, such as the monasteries of Batalha and Alcobaça.

Street scene in Baixa

UPPER AND LOWER DISTRICTS

For the visitor, one of the high points, literally and figuratively, is St George's Castle, perched on top of Lisbon's loftiest hill. From its ramparts, the castle overlooks Lisbon's oldest and most picturesque neighbourhood, Alfama. This working-class quarter, once home to the city's elite, survived the tremendous earthquake of 1755 (see page 19), and retains the labyrinthine layout of the Moors, as well as a remarkable village-like atmosphere.

To the west is the residential suburb of Belém, the city's most monumental district. It proclaims Portugal's Golden Age of Discovery with the finest Manueline monuments.

The centre of the city is the Baixa – 'lower', downtown Lisbon, a commercial waterfront district of neoclassical buildings, the old stock exchange and government ministries, quaint shops and grand squares. Most of the Baixa was lost to the natural disaster, an earthquake in 1755, but was quickly and elegantly rebuilt on a grid pattern.

The upper city, the Bairro Alto, is reached by tram, lift or steep climb. One of Lisbon's quintessential neighbourhoods, it is home to much of the city's nightlife, including *fado* houses, restaurants and bars. Within the upper city is the chic district of Chiado. Though much of it was razed in 1988 by a devastating fire, it has been impeccably rebuilt.

Renovation work that began in the late 20th century has turned the city once again towards the river and the sea. The transport infrastructure continues to be improved. Old quays and warehouses have been transformed into trendy restaurants and hot nightspots, and the Parque das Nações has added interest upriver to the east of the city.

AROUND THE CITY

Monuments to former splendours, and cutting-edge museums are not the end of the capital's charms. Lisbon is surrounded by some of Portugal's most appealing spots. To the northwest, Sintra is a magical place, with palaces and *quintas* (estates) studding beautiful pine-clad hills with views of the coast. To the west are the sparkling beach resorts of the Estoril Coast, while over the Tagus to the south are the wild Serra da Arrábida and the fishing town of Sesimbra. Closer to the capital, the handsome Versailles-style palace at Queluz is another major draw for visitors.

In the Parque das Nações

HISTORY AND CULTURE

Though a legend claims Odysseus as Lisbon's founding father, most hard-headed historians date the city's origins to around 1200BC, with the establishment of a Phoenician trading station. Its name then was Alis Ubbo or Olisipo.

People had settled in the area thousands of years before, attracted to its location on a calm river close to the Atlantic Ocean. Around 700BC, Celtic tribes moved into northern and central Portugal, while the coastal settlements were incorporated into the empire of Carthage.

Recorded history of the city begins in 205BC, when the Romans ousted the Carthaginians and created the province of Lusitania, though not without fierce resistance from the Celts. Olisipo was proclaimed a municipality and later renamed Felicitas Julia – the Joy of Julius – by Julius Caesar. The Romans built roads, cultivated grapes, wheat and olives, and bequeathed the foundations of the Portuguese language. As the power of Rome declined, most of the Iberian Peninsula was overrun by tribes from north of the Pyrenees. Lisbon fell at the beginning of the 5th century AD, after which successive migratory tribes controlled the city until the 6th century, when the Visigoths brought a period of peace.

THE MOORISH CONQUEST

In 711, 79 years after the death of the Prophet Mohammed, a fleet of ships from North Africa crossed the Strait of Gibraltar, and in just a few years the Moors had conquered most of Iberia. Lisbon became a thriving outpost under Muslim rule. Its castle, begun by the Visigoths, was enlarged, and beneath it, stretching down to the river, the narrow streets of Alfama were infused with an Arabic flavour that remains to this day.

Christians had maintained a precarious foothold in northern Portugal, but it was not until 1139, when Dom Afonso Henriques declared himself the first king of Portugal, that their struggle to gain power met with some success, defeating the Moors at the Battle of Ourique. In 1147 the king recruited a volunteer force from thousands of Flemish, Norman, German and English crusaders on their way to the Holy Land, persuading them to fight against the Moors in return for whatever booty Lisbon had to offer. The successful siege of Lisbon lasted four months. A century later the reconquest of Portugal was complete and Afonso III (1248–79) chose Lisbon as his capital.

THE GOLDEN AGE

In a decisive battle, fought in 1385 at Aljubarrota (100km/62 miles north of Lisbon), João of Avis, recently proclaimed João I of Portugal, secured independence from Spain. A new alliance with England was sealed in the 1386 Treaty of Windsor, outlining true and eternal friendship. A year later King João married Philippa of Lancaster, the daughter of John of Gaunt. Their third surviving son,

INÊS AND PEDRO

Inês de Castro and Pedro the Just are two tragic figures who could have served as the models for Shakespeare's Romeo and Juliet. Pedro, heir to the throne, defied his family and lived for a decade with the Spanish beauty, one of his queen's ladies-in-waiting. In 1355, three noblemen slit Inês's throat – a political assassination ordered by Prince Pedro's own father, Afonso IV. When he became king just two years later, Pedro exhumed her body, crowned it, and ordered all the nobles to kneel and kiss the skeleton's hand. Pedro and Inês are entombed together in the monastery at Alcobaça.

Henry the Navigator redrew
the map of the world

Henrique, Duke of Viseu, Master of the Order of Christ, became 'Henry the Navigator', who redrew the map of the world.

Prince Henry won his spurs in 1415 at the age of 21, when he sailed from Lisbon in a daring expedition to capture the North African stronghold of Ceuta. It was his first and last act of bravado, for he then retired to the 'end of the world', the Sagres peninsula in the Algarve, where he established a centre of research that gathered together astronomers, cartographers and other scientists whose work magnified the skills of mariners. Their expeditions redefined European understanding of the world. During Henry's lifetime, Portuguese caravels sailed far beyond the westernmost point of Africa. With the colonisation of the Atlantic islands of Madeira and the Azores, the foundations of the future Portuguese empire were laid.

The king who ruled over Portugal's Golden Age of Exploration – and exploitation – was Manuel I, 'The Fortunate', who reigned

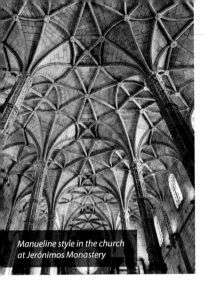

Manueline style in the church at Jerónimos Monastery

from 1495 to 1521. Discoveries made during this period made him one of Europe's richest rulers. During his reign the Tower of Belém and the impressive Jerónimos Monastery were built in the 'Manueline' architectural style that eased Portugal from the Gothic into the Renaissance. Whimsically flamboyant and decorative, it is rife with references to the sea.

The most significant expedition under Manuel's flag was Vasco da Gama's sea voyage from Lisbon in the summer of 1497. Rounding what is now known as the Cape of Good Hope, Vasco da Gama found what Columbus had been looking for but missed the sea route to the spices of the East. Reaching Calicut in southern India the following year, Portugal put an end to the Venetian monopoly of the Eastern spice trade by assuming control of the Indian Ocean and attracting merchants from all over Europe to Lisbon. Further territories were discovered in 1500, when the Portuguese explorer Pedro Álvares Cabral reached Brazil.

TIMES OF TRIAL

When Manuel died, in 1521, he was succeeded by his son, João the Pious. With one eye on the ungodly ways of prosperous Lisbon and the other on the Inquisition in Spain, João invited the Jesuits to cross the border into Portugal.

Although the Inquisition in Portugal was never as powerful as it was in Spain, it persecuted 'New Christians' – Jews who were all forced to embrace Christianity, including Spanish Jews who had been promised refuge in Portugal. Despite these witch-hunts, an outbreak of plague and such natural calamities as earthquakes, by the end of the 16th century Lisbon had an estimated population of 100,000.

When Dom Henrique died leaving no heir in 1580, Philip II of Spain marched in and forced the union of the two crowns. It took 60 years for the local forces to organise a successful uprising against the occupation. On 1 December 1640 – celebrated as Portugal's Restoration Day – Spanish rule was finally overthrown, and the Duke of Bragança was crowned João IV in a joyful ceremony in Lisbon's huge riverfront square, the Terreiro do Paço, known today as the Praça do Comércio.

His grandson, João V, enjoyed a long and glittering reign, from 1706 to 1750. As money poured in from gold discovered in Brazil, the king squandered it on lavish monuments and buildings. His greatest extravagance was the palace and monastery at Mafra, 40km (25 miles) northwest of the capital.

DESTRUCTION AND REBUILDING

The great divide between Portugal's early history and modern times falls around the middle of the 18th century when, on All Saints' Day, 1 November 1755, as the crowds packed the churches to honour the dead, Lisbon was devastated by one of the worst earthquakes ever recorded. Churches crumbled, the waters of the Tagus heaved into a tidal wave and fires spread throughout the city. The triple disaster is estimated to have killed between 15,000 and 60,000. Reminders of the nightmare are still found across Lisbon; the most evocative is the shell of the Carmelite church in the Bairro Alto district behind the Elevador de Santa

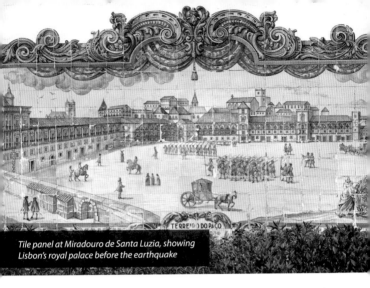

Tile panel at Miradouro de Santa Luzia, showing Lisbon's royal palace before the earthquake

Justa, which has been open to the sky since the morning its roof fell in.

Routine problems of state were beyond the talents of the ineffectual José I (1750–77), who could not be expected to cope with the challenge of post-quake recovery. The task of rebuilding fell to the power behind the throne – a tough, ambitious and tyrannical minister, Sebastião José de Carvalho e Melo, later Count of Oeiras, but best remembered as the Marquês de Pombal. Taking advantage of the power vacuum once the earth had stopped shaking, he mobilised all of Portugal's resources for the clean-up. Survivors were fed and housed, corpses disposed of, ruins cleared and an ambitious project for a newly structured city laid out.

Today, the modern sections of the capital are aptly referred to as 'Pombaline Lisbon'. Pombal's achievements are commemorated with his heroic statue, on top of a column at the north end of the Avenida da Liberdade in downtown Lisbon, a central road hub referred to as 'Pombal'. A huge equestrian statue of José holds the main place of honour in the Praça do Comércio, where the riverside royal palace had been before the earthquake. The king had a close brush with death in an assassination attempt in 1758, after which Pombal inaugurated a reign of terror, with widespread repression.

PENINSULAR WAR AND CIVIL WAR

At the beginning of the 19th century, Napoleon managed to drag Portugal into the heat of Europe's conflicts. The situation became so perilous that the royal family fled to Brazil on board British ships. Taking no chances, they remained there until 1821, 10 years after the crisis was over.

In 1807 Napoleon had tried to pressure Portugal into abandoning its traditional loyalty to England. Lisbon attempted to stay neutral, but when it refused to declare war on Britain, the French army under General Andoche Junot marched in, setting up headquarters in the Queluz Palace, just outside Lisbon.

Military miscalculations in the face of a British expedition sent Junot's army packing in 1808. Over the next few years, repeat engagements became notable victories for the combined Portuguese-British forces, largely thanks to the strategic tactics of

AZULEJOS

Azulejos, the hand-painted, glazed ceramic tiles omnipresent in Lisbon, are not merely decorative. After the Great Earthquake and fires devastated much of Lisbon and the surrounding area in the 18th century, these tiles were widely used to protect buildings from going up in flames again. The name *azulejo* is thought to be derived from *al-zuleiq*, Arabic for small polished stone. At the Museu Nacional do Azulejo you can see how they are made.

Statue of Pedro IV in the Rossio

the British commander, Sir Arthur Wellesley (later the Duke of Wellington). After the textbook battle of the Lines of Torres Vedras, north of Lisbon, the French began a long retreat, sacking and looting as they went. Their last outpost in Portugal was evacuated in 1811.

Peace was still to prove elusive, and 17 years later the country was again at war – this time pitting brother against brother. On the death of João VI, his eldest son, Pedro IV, who had become emperor of a newly independent Brazil, fought to wrest the crown of Portugal from his absolutist brother, Miguel I. Pedro won, though he died of consumption only months later, in September 1834, aged 36. His adolescent daughter, Maria da Glória, assumed the throne. She married the German nobleman Ferdinand of Saxe-Coburg-Gotha, who built for her the astonishing Pena Palace above Sintra and fathered her five sons and six daughters. Maria II died in childbirth at the age of 34.

Premature and tragic deaths claimed many Portuguese royals, but in all the country's history only one king was assassinated. On 1 February 1908, as the royal family was riding in an open carriage past the Terreiro do Paço, an assassin's bullet felled Carlos I. A few seconds later another conspirator fatally shot Carlos's son and heir, Prince Luís Felipe. A third bullet hit the young prince Manuel in the arm. Thus wounded and haunted, Manuel II began a brief two-year reign as Portugal's last king. He was deposed on 5 October 1910 in a republican uprising supported by certain elements of the armed forces. The royal yacht spirited him to Gibraltar and later to England, where he lived in exile.

REPUBLIC TO DICTATORSHIP

The republican form of government was as unstable as it was unfamiliar. Resignations, coups and assassinations kept an unhappy merry-go-round of presidents and prime ministers whirling. The nation could ill afford a war, but German threats to its African territories pushed Portugal towards World War I on the side of the Allies.

The war's toll hastened the end of Portugal's unsuccessful attempt at democracy. After a revolution in 1926, General António Óscar Carmona assumed control, and two years later entrusted the economy to António de Oliveira Salazar, then an economics professor at Coimbra University. The exhausted Portuguese finances rallied soon afterwards. In 1932 Salazar was named prime minister. His tough, authoritarian regime – the Estado Novo (New State) – favoured economic progress and nationalism. He kept Portugal neutral in World War II, but permitted the Allies to use the Azores as a base.

THE CARNATION REVOLUTION

When Salazar suffered a stroke in 1968, power was handed to Dr Marcelo Caetano. However, in 1974 the armed forces, discontented by hopeless colonial wars, overthrew the dictatorship in the so-called Carnation Revolution. Portugal disengaged itself from Mozambique and Angola, and managed to absorb the million or so refugees who fled to a motherland most had never seen. The nation suffered several years of political confusion and great hardship before adjusting to democracy.

With entry into the European Union in 1986, development quickened, and Portugal soon had one of Europe's fastest-growing economies. As host of World Expo in 1998, Lisbon launched a gleaming new neighbourhood, Parque das Nações, east of the city. That year also saw the writer José Saramago win the Nobel Prize for Literature. In 2004 Portugal hosted the European Football Championship, for which new stadiums were built and others renovated.

But the economy began to stagnate and the 2008 financial crisis left Portugal with a budget deficit that was fast spiralling out of control. In 2011, it became the third EU country after Greece and Ireland to ask for a financial bail-out from the EU. It wasn't until 2014, after harsh austerity measures had been implemented and the budget deficit reduced, that Portugal exited the bailout programme. Recent years have seen the gradual elimination of austerity measures by the socialist-led government, currently headed by António Costa, and a steady economic revival as well as a decrease in unemployment.

Like countries the world over, Portugal suffered economically during the Covid-19 pandemic, but its economy has recovered better than other European countries, largely thanks to a resurgent tourism industry.

Lisbon of the future at Belem's Maat

HISTORICAL LANDMARKS

c.1200BC Phoenicians establish Alis Ubbo or Olisipo trading post.

c.700BC Celtic tribes arrive.

205BC Romans create Lusitania; Olisipo is made a municipality.

5th century AD After the decline of Rome, Visigoths settle in Lisbon.

711 Moors arrive on the peninsula and swiftly conquer it.

883 Northern Portugal (Portucale) regained by Christian forces.

1139 Dom Afonso Henríques declares himself first king of Portugal.

1255 Capital of Portugal transferred from Coimbra to Lisbon.

1386 Treaty of Windsor confirms England–Portugal alliance.

1415 Explorers reach Madeira, starting the Age of Discoveries.

1498 Vasco da Gama opens a sea route to India.

1500 Pedro Álvares Cabral reaches Brazil.

1580 Portugal falls under Spanish rule for 60 years.

1755 The Great Earthquake devastates Lisbon.

1807 Napoleonic troops invade Portugal during the Peninsular War.

1828–34 Civil war between Pedro IV and Miguel I.

1908 Carlos I and Prince Luís Felipe assassinated.

1916 Germany declares war on Portugal.

1932 António de Oliveira Salazar becomes prime minister.

1974 The Carnation Revolution restores democracy; Portugal pulls out of African colonies and a million expatriates return.

1986 Portugal joins the European Union.

2001 The euro replaces the escudo as the national currency.

2011 Portuguese negotiate an economic bailout from the EU, harsh austerity measures are introduced.

2014 End of the EU/IMF bailout programme, beginning of the economic recovery.

2016 Social democrat Marcelo Rebelo de Sousa becomes president.

2017 Wildfires ravage vast swathes of Portugal killing over 100 people.

2020 The first case of Covid-19 is recorded in March.

2022 Portugal's Cristiano Ronaldo became the only male footballer ever to score a goal in five separate World Cup competitions.

Padrão dos Descobrimentos

OUT AND ABOUT

Lisbon's waterfront is an arc stretching nearly 32km (20 miles) along the River Tagus. At the western end is Belém and at the eastern extreme is the Parque das Nações, the site of Expo 98. A city map shows that many of the top attractions in Lisbon are within walking distance of the river, but because of the hills and the way in which the sights are spread out, it isn't always very easy to go directly from one to another.

As in many cities, it's best to organise your time and interests according to neighbourhood. The Belém district on the west side of the city holds several of the star visitor attractions, but the central areas, such as Alfama and the Bairro Alto either side of the Baixa, are better for dining, shopping and lingering.

You can travel cheaply and efficiently from place to place by public transport. Buses are quick and straightforward; antique trams ply routes around the old town; and funiculars make light work of steep hills. Lisbon's Metro system is modern and fast, with further expansion underway. Taxis are plentiful and fairly inexpensive. Parking is usually difficult or even impossible on weekdays, so a car is best saved for out-of-town excursions.

On arrival, a guided city tour, whether by bus or ferry along the river, can be a good way to grasp the general layout (see page 122).

ALFAMA

Alfama is Lisbon's oldest, most picturesque and most

The Tagus

The River Tagus (Tejo) is 940km (585 miles) long, rising in Spain (where it is known as the Rio Tajo), and passing through Toledo. Its delta, to the south of Lisbon, is an important wildlife area.

fascinating area. Here, in a labyrinth of steep, crooked streets, alleys and stairways – a layout left by Moorish occupants of the city – little seems to have changed since the Middle Ages. The whole area between the castle and the waterfront is a jumble of tilting houses with peeling paint, laundry hanging from windows, bars and fish stalls. The streets are so narrow that it's not uncommon to overhear elderly women sharing gossip across balconies.

You are almost certain to get lost, but in this area – safe and easy-going by day – that's part of the attraction. Stick to the narrow streets; if you find yourself in a street wide enough for two cars to pass, then you have strayed from the Alfama area.

A good start to your explorations is at the bottom of the hill at the **Museu do Fado** ❶ (Fado Museum; www.museudofado.pt; Tue–Sun 10am–6pm) in Largo do Chafariz de Dentro. This sets the tone for the soul of the district, with a history of the city's famous music in song sheets, film clips and recordings, and a complete mocked-up *fado* tavern where you can sit and listen to Amália Rodrigues and other bygone stars, then select a souvenir from the CDs on sale.

Nearby is the **Museu do Teatro Romano** (Roman Theatre Museum; Rua de São Mamede, 3 A; www.museudelisboa.pt; Tue–Sun 10am–6pm), the contemporary home of a ruined Roman theatre that was buried in the 1755 earthquake and excavated in 1964.

Trams to Alfama

Taking a tram is the best way to get up into Alfama: No. 12 goes from Praça da Figueira and No. 28 from Bairro Alto. They share the same tracks in Alfama and you won't get lost if you follow their iron rails.

MIRADOUROS

Alternatively, take the easier path into Alfama, with a tram to one of its vantage points, and let gravity lead you back

Miradouro de Santa Luzia

down towards the river. The **Miradouro de Santa Luzia** ❷ is one such bluff on the edge of Alfama. From a pretty balcony covered with painted tiles and bougainvillea there are stunning views over a jumble of tiled roofs that cascade down to the river. Tourists mix with old men in black berets playing cards and chatting. Two detailed and dramatic azulejos (tile panels) on the wall facing the belvedere show Lisbon's waterfront as it was before the Great Earthquake and, in bloodthirsty detail, the rout of the Moors from the castle.

Just up the street is another terrific *miradouro* (lookout point), with even more expansive views. A small café on **Largo das Portas do Sol** serves snacks and beverages; visitors have been known to remain here for hours on end.

Between the two, and just above the Miradouro de Santa Luzia, the fine 17th-century **Azurara Palace** has been filled with magnificent pieces of furniture, Chinese porcelain, a priceless

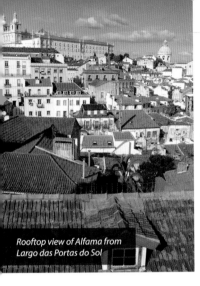

Rooftop view of Alfama from Largo das Portas do Sol

silver collection, and several tapestries from 16th- to 19th-century Portugal and its colonies, forming the **Museu de Artes Decorativas** (Decorative Arts Museum; Wed–Mon 10am–5pm; www.fress.pt). The museum belongs to the Ricardo do Espírito Santo Silva Foundation, which was established in the 1950s by the eponymous banker and displays his valuable collection. The Foundation has 18 workshops where artisans practice traditional crafts such as woodwork, metalwork, gilding and bookbinding.

ALFAMA GEMS

Some of Alfama's lesser-known attractions are best stumbled across by accident, through an arch or around a blind corner. Here is a selection of them.

Rua de São João da Praça is where the first king of Portugal, Dom Afonso Henriques, entered Lisbon through the Moorish defensive wall on 25 October 1147. The remains of a tower that was part of the Moorish defences can be found on **Largo de São Rafael**.

Rua de São Pedro is one of Alfama's lively shopping streets. On weekdays, it's filled with a mix of gossiping shoppers, café tables spilling out onto the road, dogs and children playing football.

Igreja de São Miguel (St Michael's Church) was built in the 12th century and restored after the earthquake; it has a glorious ceiling of Brazilian jacaranda wood and a rococo gilt altar screen. To the east, **Igreja de Santo Estêvão** (St Stephen's Church) has a 13th-century octagonal floor plan, but has been rebuilt several times over the years; the overhanging back of the church nearly collides with the front gate of an old palace.

The alley called **Beco da Cardosa**, with its blind-alley offshoots, is the very essence of Alfama's appeal. On **Beco do Carneiro** (Sheep Alley), ancient houses sag towards each other across a stepped-street barely wide enough for two people; above, the eaves of the buildings actually touch.

SÃO VICENTE DE FORA AND THE PANTEÃO NACIONAL

Just beyond the dense quarters of the Alfama, but linked to the neighbourhood, are two of its top sights. Though you might have trouble navigating the crooked streets up to it, the twin towers of the **Igreja e Mosteiro de São Vicente de Fora** ❸ (Church

ST VINCENT OF LISBON

The remains of St Vincent are kept in a beautiful silver reliquary at São Vicente de Fora. Vincent was martyred at Valencia in 336, but when the Moors took that city in the 8th century the inhabitants fled by sea, taking the relics of St Vincent with them. They were driven ashore on the coast of Algarve at the cape now known as Cape St Vincent, and there the relics remained until Dom Afonso Henriques had them brought to the capital and deposited in the church he had just built. Two ravens faithfully escorted the saintly relics, which explains why many a Lisbon lamp-post bears the symbol of a sailing ship with a bird fore and aft.

Thieves' Market

Behind São Vicente, around the Mercado Santa Clara, Alfama's colourful *Feira da Ladra* (Thieves' Market) is held every Tuesday and Saturday from dawn to dusk.

and Monastery of St Vincent Beyond the Walls), rising above a hillside east of the São Jorge castle, are impossible to miss. Founded by Dom Afonso Henriques immediately after retaking the city from the Moors (tombs of the Teutonic knights who helped him lie beneath the Sacristy), it was reconstructed in the 16th century around the time of the Inquisition. This huge Italianate building succeeds in combining substance with grace. The entrance to the **monastery** (Tues–Sun 10am–6pm) is on the right, where there is a pleasant café.

Built over an enormous cistern, many of the monastery's walls and courtyards are lined with *azulejos*, though the *Fables* of La Fontaine, depicted in 38 *azulejo* tableaux, have been removed and repositioned for display on the first floor. An exhibition explains the history of the Patriarchate of Lisbon, granted by the Pope in 1720, and pantheons contain tombs of the patriarchs and of Bragança royalty, including Catherine of Bragança, queen of Charles II of England, and Carlos I and his heir Prince Luís Felipe, assassinated together in 1908.

A further pantheon, the **Panteão Nacional** ❹ (Igreja de Santa Engrácia; Tues–Sun 10am–5pm; closes at 6pm from April to September); www.panteaonacional.gov.pt) is the other dominant building in the area, just downhill from the monastery. This grandiosely domed marble church was begun in the 17th century, but the final touch, the cupola, wasn't completed until 1966. To describe something as the 'works of Santa Engrácia' is to call it an endless task.

Santa Engrácia remained a church until a few years ago, when it was deconsecrated and became the national pantheon, honouring great figures in Portuguese history with symbolic tombs in the sumptuous rotunda. To one side are the real tombs of presidents of the republic and contributors to Portuguese culture, including the famous *fado* singer Amália Rodrigues (1920–99), which always has fresh flowers. You can climb to the gallery for a view onto the marble floor of the rotunda, and to the terrace and dome, though there is often a queue for the lift.

THE CASTLE

Almost every hill in this elevated part of town has a *miradouro*, but the best panorama of all belongs to the **Castelo de São Jorge** ❺ (St George's Castle; www.castelodesaojorge.pt; daily 9am–7pm,

The Castelo de São Jorge

The facade of Sé Patriarcal

in summer until 9, camera obscura 10am–1pm, in summer open until 3pm), which is reached by the steep alley and steps that continue up from the tram stop on Rua de Santa Justa. From the ramparts, you can look out across the centre of Lisbon, over the Baixa to the Bairro Alto, down to the river and the Ponte 25 de Abril, as far as Belém.

The Moors, who ruled Portugal between the 8th and 12th centuries, clung hard to their castle but were finally dislodged in 1147. The new proprietor, Dom Afonso Henriques, expanded the fortifications, but earthquakes as well as general wear and tear over the following centuries left little intact. Restoration has since given new life to the old ruins, even if that means that much of the castle is not original.

Apart from the sensational vistas and the chance to roam the battlements, the castle is worth a visit for the park gardens inside its walls. Peacocks and other birds strut around as if they own the place. Also inside is **an archeological exhibition** and the camera obscura, with a system of lenses and mirrors that provide views of the city.

THE CATHEDRAL

Many cities tend to be built around their grand cathedral squares, but Lisbon's cathedral, **Sé Patriarcal** ❻, (Lisbon Cathedral;

Nov–April Mon–Sat 9am–6pm; May–Oct Mon, Tues, Thurs & Fri 9.30am–7pm, Wed & Sat 10am–6pm; closed Sundays and holy days), appears out of nowhere at a bend in the road. It is most easily reached from the centre by continuing east on the extension of Rua da Conceição. Despite the lack of pomp and circumstance, this handsome building has significant historic and artistic importance. Begun as a fortress-church in the 12th century, its towers and walls suggest a citadel. The church suffered earthquake damage during the 14th, 16th and 18th centuries, but it retains its Romanesque facade. The 13th-century cloister gardens have been excavated to reveal signs of Iron Age, Roman and Moorish occupation all on this same site. A **Roman amphitheatre** has been uncovered just above the site.

A few steps down the hill from the cathedral, the little **Igreja de Santo António da Sé** (www.stoantoniolisboa.com), built in 1812, honours Lisbon's revered native son, known throughout the world as St Anthony of Padua. The crypt – all that survived the 1755 earthquake – was built on the spot where, according to local lore, St Anthony's house stood. He is the patron saint of women looking for husbands; sometimes, bridal bouquets are left at his altar in the cathedral, along with thanks for all of his good work. It's worth looking in the Santo António Museum (www.museude lisboa.pt; Tue–Sun 10am–6pm) next to the church.

Towards the waterfront, at Campo das Cebolas, the **Casa dos Bicos,** faced with sharp pyramid-shaped stones, dates from the early 16th century. It belonged to the illegitimate son of Afonso de Albuquerque, the viceroy of Portuguese India. It is now the seat of the **José Saramago Foundation** (www.josesaramago.org), a private institution dedicated to the life and work of José Saramago, Portugal's first Literature Nobel Prize winner. On the ground floor of the building is a museum where you can see the archeological ruins beneath the building and view finds that were dug up there,

Casa dos Bicos

some more than 2000 years old (www.museudelisboa.pt Tue–Sat 10am–6pm).

The **Rua dos Bacalhoeiros** (Street of Cod-Sellers), on which the house stands, has various small but worthwhile *tascas* (restaurants) and the Loja dos Descobrimentos handicraft shop (www.loja-descobrimentos.com), specialising in hand-painted tiles. The west end of the street leads to the large waterfront square, Praça do Comércio, one of the largest in Portugal.

A DETOUR EAST: TWO MUSEUMS

Along the riverfront just to the east of Alfama are two important museums. The **Museu Militar** (Military Museum; www.exercito.pt; Tue–Sun 10am–5pm), in a large building across the square from the Santa Apolónia railway station, is on the site of a foundry where cannon were cast during the 16th century. Among the exhibits is Vasco da Gama's two-handed sword, almost as tall as a man, relics of the Napoleonic Wars and mementoes of Portugal's last skirmishes in its colonies.

A short way beyond is the marvellous, light-filled **Museu Nacional do Azulejo ❼** (National Tile Museum; Tue–Sun 10am–6pm), devoted entirely to the art of the painted ceramic tiles that are on view everywhere in Portugal. The museum occupies much of the former Manueline Convento da Madre de Deus (1509), and includes a small double-decker cloister surrounded by tiles in Moorish-style geometric patterns. It is filled with around 12,000 beautiful *azulejos*, ranging from 15th-century polychrome designs to contemporary examples.

One treasure is the *Lisbon Panorama*, a 36m- (118ft-) long composition of blue-and-white painted tiles, recording Lisbon's riverside as it looked 25 years before the 1755 earthquake. Another is the fabulous interior of the small church of Igreja da Madre de Deus, an interesting mix of rococo gilt and gorgeous *azulejos*. Side walls are adorned with blue-and-white tiles from The Netherlands; two rows of enormous paintings hang above them, and the ceiling also serves as a giant canvas.

BAIXA (LOWER CITY)

Praça do Comércio ❽ (Commerce Square) is a rare extravagant touch in understated Lisbon. Stately arcades and bold yellow government buildings line three sides of the vast square; the fourth is open to the river, with Venetian-style marble steps leading down to the water. On the east side of the steps is the Terreiro do Paço terminal for ferries to the opposite shore (see page 122). Ferries also leave from Cais do Sodré to the west.

Museu Nacional do Azulejo

Foodies' paradise

The city's main market, Mercado da Ribeira is now home to the Time Out Market (www.timeout market.com/lisboa; Sun–Thurs 10am–midnight, Fri & Sat till 1am), a foodies' paradise where some of the best chefs in Portugal have stalls, including Henrique Sá Pessoa and Marlene Vieira. Or you can simply choose a drink, a pastry or lunch from any of the stalls and eat it at the communal central tables.

Terreiro do Paço (Palace Square) was the name of this square during the four centuries when the Royal Ribeira Palace stood here, and many *Lisboetas* still use this name today, but the 1755 earthquake wiped out the entire complex of palatial buildings. The post-quake layout is harmonious and stately, but it remains part of many citizens' daily lives. They catch buses and trams here, while children play around temporary exhibitions and installations.

The Praça do Comércio has been the backdrop for some of history's dramas: King Carlos I and his son were killed here by an assassin in 1908, and this is where the first uprising of the Carnation Revolution of 1974 was staged.

The city's main tourist office, the **Lisboa Welcome Centre** (www.visitlisboa.com) is on Praça do Comércio, on the opposite side to the **Lisboa Story Centre** (www.lisboastorycentre.pt; daily 10am–5pm), a fun audio-visual exhibition of the city's history. In the middle of the square is the bronze equestrian statue of José I, patron of the Marquês de Pombal, who designed the square as the centrepiece of his post-earthquake reconstruction. Another sculptural flourish is the triumphal arch, depicting the Marquês de Pombal and the explorer Vasco da Gama, and connecting government buildings on the north of the square.

The huge **Arco da Rua Augusta** (daily 10am–7pm), which you can go up for great views over the square, leads to the pedestrianised **Rua Augusta**, the main thoroughfare of Pombal's 18th-century grid and an attractive shopping street. Tiled façades and Art Nouveau touches are a feature of these 15 earthquake-proof side streets, which are full of intriguing shops, banks and small restaurants. The parallel Rua de Prata and Rua do Ouro (Silver and Gold Streets) are named after the original specialist shops in the area.

At No. 24 lies the exceptional **MUDE-Museu do Design e da Moda ❾** (Design and Fashion Museum; www.mude.pt; currently closed for renovation), Europe's leading museum of 20th-century design. It contains an incredible collection of furniture, industrial design and couture, including items by Charles Eames, Frank Gehry, Phillipe Starck, Balenciaga and Yves Saint Laurent.

On the west side of the Baixa is the Bairro Alto, the 'Upper Quarter', which is easily scaled by the **Elevador de Santa Justa ❿** (daily 7.30am–9pm, in summer until 11pm; viewing platform 9am–9pm, in summer until 11pm; www.carris.pt), a 30m- (100ft-) high iron neo-Gothic lift built by Raúl Mesnier in 1902. Originally powered by steam, it was rebuilt in 1993. An upper gangway gives access to the Bairro Alto. Today the still-functioning lift takes people to the level just below the top, from where a spiral staircase leads up to

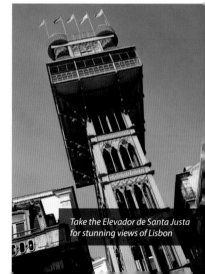

Take the Elevador de Santa Justa for stunning views of Lisbon

the main observation deck, with its pleasant café and sensational views of Lisbon's tiled rooftops and the São Jorge castle.

The steps behind the lift lead up to emerge at the gently sloping **Rua do Carmo**, with a blend of modern and traditional shops. The latter include the **Luvaria Ulisses** (www.luvariaulisses.com), a glove shop with an Art-Deco street frontage that is barely a metre wide.

ROSSIO

Turn left up Rua do Carmo to enter the Chiado district (see page 45), or follow it down to the right to emerge on the **Rossio** ⑪ (formally named Praça Dom Pedro IV), Lisbon's main square, once the scene of public hangings, bullfights and the burning of the Inquisition's victims. Today, the square is still one of the main centres of activity in Lisbon – it's a great place to window-shop, meet friends, watch the busy crowds go by from pavement cafés, such as the Art Nouveau **Nicola**, and listen to the fountains.

The statue on the column in the square honours the first emperor of Brazil, Pedro IV (1826–34). On the northern end of the square is the handsome **Teatro Nacional Dona Maria II** (www.tndm.pt). Just beyond the theatre on the right are a couple of *ginjinha* (cherry brandy) kiosks, which make the area an evening gathering place. Nearby is the southern end of **Rua das Portas de Santo Antão**, a street bustling with lively restaurant tables, much appreciated by patrons of the popular **Teatro Politeama** up on the left. At No. 58 is the **Casa do Alentejo**. Once the property of the counts of Alverca, it is unassuming from the outside, but as you go through the entrance and up the steps you're confronted by a riot of interior styling: an attractive Moorish courtyard with Art Deco flourishes, and on the first floor, a traditional restaurant with massed panels of vivid *azulejos*, serving excellent Alentejo dishes at reasonable prices.

On the west side of the square, one street removed, is the **Estação do Rossio**, the railway station from where local trains run to Sintra and Mafra (see pages 66 and 71). Its horseshoe arches make it look like a Moorish palace, but it is a romantic effort of the late 19th century.

To the east of Rossio is another major square, **Praça da Figueira**, which is another hub for buses and the No. 12 tram. At its centre is a statue of João I, founder of the Avis dynasty. Just to the northeast is **Praça Martim Moniz**, decked with fountains that function as a water park for children. The views of Alfama and the castle district from here are lovely.

The road past Rossio station opens out into **Praça dos Restauradores** (Square of the Restoration), where an obelisk celebrates the overthrow of Spanish rule in 1640. **Palácio Foz**, the once splendid pink palace on the west side of the square beside the former Art Deco Teatro Eden, now houses a **tourist information**

Praça dos Restauradores

office Ask me Lisboa (www.visitlisboa.com; daily 10am–6.30pm). Just beyond it, the Elevador da Glória funicular takes you up to the Bairro Alto (see page 42).

From this point, **Avenida da Liberdade** makes its way uphill for a little over 1km (0.5 mile). The stately boulevard of upmarket shops is graced with statues, fountains, ponds, flower gardens, promenade cafés and benches. The boulevard ends at the **Praça Marquês de Pombal** (or Rotunda) traffic hub from which an elevated statue of Pombal, accompanied by a lion, looks out over his rebuilt Lisbon.

BAIRRO ALTO (UPPER CITY)

Like the steep Alfama district, the Bairro Alto is a hilly and dense area full of picturesque old houses, their wrought-iron balconies hung with birdcages and flowerpots. Half asleep during the day, Bairro Alto is the nightlife epicentre of Lisbon. After dark, the sad songs of *fado* nightclubs spill out into the cobbled streets.

The easiest way to reach the Bairro Alto is to board the **Elevador da Glória**, the yellow funicular trolley at Praça dos Restauradores. Locals, however, are as apt to walk up the steep hill as wait for the funicular. At the top end of the brief journey is a lookout park, **Miradouro de São Pedro de Alcântara**, with an excellent view of the Castelo de São Jorge across the Baixa.

Opposite the top of the funicular, on the ground floor of the 18th-century Palace of São Pedro de Alcântara, is the **Solar do Vinho do Porto** ⓬ (Port and Douro Wines Institute; www.ivdp.pt; Mon–Fri 11am–7pm), where you can sample the famous Portuguese wines.

North of the *miradouro*, along Rua de São Pedro de Alcântara, lies the **Jardim Botânico** (Botanical Garden; summer daily 10am–8pm, winter daily 10am–5pm), reached through the university gate alongside the Academy of Sciences, at Rua Escola Politécnica 58; it is part of the Museu National de História Natural e da Ciencia (www.museus.ulisboa.pt). The tree-shaded gardens slope steeply downhill and concentrate on the scientific cultivation of unusual plants from distant climes, but this serious activity doesn't disturb the lush, slightly unkempt beauty.

SÃO ROQUE AND CARMO CHURCHES

Two churches in the upper town are unusual enough to merit a visit. Just down Rua de São Pedro do Alcântara, turning left from the top of the funicular, is Largo Trindade Coelho and the **Igreja de São Roque** ⓭. The church's dull exterior (the original 16th-century façade perished in the 1755 earthquake) conceals the most lavishly decorated chapel in Lisbon: the baroque altar of the chapel of São João Baptista (St John the Baptist) is a wealth of gold, silver, bronze, agate, amethyst, lapis lazuli, ivory and Carrara marble. In 1742, João V of Portugal sent orders for this altar to Rome, where teams of artists and artisans worked on it for five years. After the Pope had given his blessing, the prefabricated masterpiece was dismantled and shipped to the customer. The church ceiling, from 1589, is the only surviving example in Lisbon of a Mannerist painted ceiling. Adjoining the church, the impressive **Museu de Arte Sacra** (Museum of Sacred Art; https://mais.scml.pt/museu-saoroque; Apr–Sep Mon

2–7pm, Tue–Sun 10am–7pm, Thurs until 8pm, Oct–Mar Mon 2–6pm, Tues–Sun 10am–6pm) contains a collection of beautifully presented precious reliquaries, paintings, delicately worked jewellery and vestments.

The Bairro Alto's restaurants and bars are in the side streets to the west of Rua de São Pedro de Alcântara. For a daylight impression of the narrow streets with their overhanging balconies, take a walk from Largo Trindade Coelho up the **Travessa da Queimada**. The streets are in a grid pattern, so it's easy to explore and navigate your way back.

From Largo Trindade Coelho, you can also walk downhill towards the Chiado district, via **Rua Nova da Trindade**. Halfway down on the left is the **Cervejeria da Trindade**, an old beer hall decorated with *azulejos*, where you can enjoy tasty Portuguese dishes and excellent seafood (see page 107).

Window shopping in Chiado

If you continue to the bottom and turn left, you'll arrive at Largo do Carmo, where the **Igreja do Carmo** 🄬 (Carmelite Church) is rich only in memories. Today it stands in ruins, a mere shell, but is an evocative reminder of the 1755 earthquake's tremendous destruction – the roof fell in on a full congregation on All Saints' Day. The foundations date to the 14th century. Housed inside the only part of the church that has a roof over it is the

Museu Archeológico do Carmo (www.museuarqueo logicodocarmo.pt; Mon–Sat 10am–6pm, May–Oct until 7pm). This small archaeological museum has a collection that includes prehistoric pottery, some Roman sculptures, early Portuguese tombs and even a few ancient mummies under glass.

'Nastiest city'

Henry Fielding's *Journal of a Voyage to Lisbon*, published just after his death in 1754, ends with his arrival at seven in the evening: 'I got into a chaise on shore, and was driven through the nastiest city in the world…'

CHIADO AND SÃO BENTO PALACE

The streets of chic **Chiado** have long been renowned for dispensing Lisbon's most elegant goods – silverware, leather, fashions and books – along with fine pastry and tea shops. The main commercial street, with some high-end fashion shops, is **Rua Garrett**, where a statue of the poet Fernando Pessoa sits outside **Café A Brasileira**, which has attracted artists for a century.

In 1988 part of Chiado was devastated by fires that wiped out two of Europe's oldest department stores, including the legendary Armazéns do Chiado (www.armazensdochiado.com). Portugal's most famous architect, the modernist Álvaro Siza, oversaw the tastefully preserved reconstruction of the neighbourhood, especially along Rua do Carmo (see page 40). On the **Largo Barão Quintela**, just off Rua do Alecrim, is another statue, this one of the 19th-century novelist Eça de Queiroz, gazing upon a naked muse.

The **Museu do Chiado** (www.museuartecontemporanea.gov.pt; Tue–Fri Sun 10am–1pm & 2–6pm, Sat & Sun 10am–2pm & 3–6pm), in the former San Francisco Convent on Rua Serpa Pinto, houses an impressive collection of Portuguese art from the late 19th century to the present.

West of the Bairro Alto lies the **Palácio São Bento**, a former Benedictine monastery that is now home to Portugal's parliament (www.en.parlamento.pt). Beyond it is the delightful park Jardim Guerra Jumqueiro, better known as **Jardim da Estrela** after the distinguished 18th-century church across the street. This richly decorated basilica was completed in 1789. The 19th-century park contains abundant tropical foliage, plus the customary ducks, geese, peacocks and pheasants. Just beyond the park is the **Cemitério dos Ingleses** (English Cemetery), where Henry Fielding (1707–54), author of *Tom Jones*, is buried.

LAPA

Moving west and down towards the river from Chiado is the elegant residential neighbourhood of Lapa. It is home to embassies, townhouses and several intimate hotels, but to most visitors it is known as the address of the **Museu Nacional de Arte Antiga** ⑮ (National Museum of Ancient Art; www.museudearteantiga. pt; Tue–Sun 10am–6pm), Portugal's most important collection of ancient art. It is housed on the site of a Carmelite convent in a large and handsomely designed palace on Rua das Janelas Verdes. On three floors, the museum is an absorbing place with at least several masterpieces of international renown.

On the ground floor (Piso 1) a whole glittering salon is dedicated to textiles and furniture, plus paintings by foreign artists, including Tiepolo, Dürer and, most strikingly, the Spaniard Francisco de Zurbarán, whose six larger-than-life saints once belonged to the monastery of São Vicente de Fora (see page 31).

The same floor also has a triptych – both entertaining and horrific – by Hieronymus Bosch (1450–1516), the Flemish artist who painted surreal allegorical scenes with alien-like creatures. *The Temptation of St Anthony*, painted around 1500, is a fantastic hallucination, tempered with humour and executed with mad genius. A crane rigged up like a helicopter, flying fish taxis and horse-size rats fill this ghoulish nightmare.

The second floor contains oriental art, much of it dating from the discoveries of the 15th and 16th centuries. Two Japanese lacquer screens depict the moment that the Portuguese – the first Europeans – landed in Japan. The new arrivals are depicted as villains up to no good, while the locals watch, amused, from their balconies.

The top floor is devoted to Portuguese art and sculpture. Here a highlight is *The Adoration of St Vincent*, a multi-panel work also taken from São Vicente de Fora monastery and attributed to the 15th-century Portuguese master, Nuno Gonçalves. It is a spectacular portrait of contemporary dignitaries, including Henry the Navigator. Dozens of others are shown in every range of *distracção* – ire, boredom and amusement – while several of the assembled clergymen appear as ugly, evil or both.

There is a pleasant garden and café, which looks out over the river and the **Doca do Alcântara**, with its waterfront bars, clubs and restaurants. The Doca is also home to the **Museu do Oriente** (www.museudo oriente.pt; Tue–Sun 10am–6pm, Fri until 8pm, free Fri 6–8pm), housed in a former

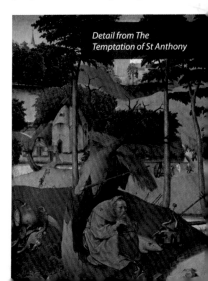

Detail from The Temptation of St Anthony

Mosteiro dos Jerónimos

fish warehouse, with an interesting collection examining Portugal's historical links with Asia.

Nearby, the quay of the smaller **Doca de Santo Amaro** yachting marina, just beneath Ponte 25 de April, is lined with restaurants.

BELÉM

Belém (Portuguese for Bethlehem), Lisbon's primary monumental district, is a suburb about 6km (4 miles) west of Praça do Comércio, where land reclaimed from the river has been fashioned into parkland, new cultural centres and marinas. Though the shoreline has changed beyond recognition, it was from here that the great Portuguese voyages of discovery set out in the 15th and 16th centuries.

Tram 15 makes the waterfront trip to Belém from Praça do Comércio; bus No. 201 from Cais do Sodré (just west of Praça do Comércio) covers virtually the same route but ends up at Linda-a-Velha.

Start a visit to Belém at the edge closest to central Lisbon.

MAAT

The newest addition to the riverside is the ultramodern wave-like organic building of the **Museum of Art, Architecture and Technology** ⑯ (MAAT; www.maat.pt; Wed–Mon 11am–7pm) designed by the British architect Amanda Levete. It exhibits the work of contemporary artists, architects and the treasures of the EDP Foundation's Art Collection. The museum also includes the complex of the Tejo Power Station with fine examples of the last century industrial architecture and the interesting Electricity Museum. Even if you don't want to go inside the gallery, it's worth walking over roof of the building for great river views.

MUSEU NACIONAL DOS COCHES

The interesting **Museu Nacional dos Coches** (National Coach Museum; http://museudoscoches.gov.pt; main building Tue–Sun 10am–6pm; Old Riding School Wed–Mon 10am–6pm) is housed in the former riding school of the Belém Royal Palace and a new building designed by the Pritzker Prize winner, Brazilian architect Paulo Mendes da Rocha (2015). It displays dozens of impressive carriages, drawn by royal horses for ceremonial occasions over four centuries, both in the city and across the country. The most extravagant are three sculpted, gilt carriages used by the Portuguese Embassy in Rome in the early 18th century. The bulk of the collection is in the new building, so if you're pushed for the time this is the one to chose.

PALÁCIO DA AJUDA

A short distance away, on the Calçada da Ajuda, sits the rose-coloured official residence of the president of the Republic, **Palácio da Ajuda** ⓱ (https://culturaportugal. gov.pt/en/conhecer/places/_ dgpc/palacio-nacional-da-ajuda; Thu–Tue 10am–6pm), the biggest palace inside the

Custard tarts

The Belém district is famous for its special pastries (*pastéis de Belém*) – warm custard tarts dusted with icing sugar and cinnamon. The best, made to a secret recipe, are those sold at the Pastéis de Belém (see page 110), at Rua de Belém, No. 84–92.

city limits. Work began on the former royal residence in 1802 to replace the temporary wooden palace erected here after the earthquake. Soon after, in 1807, the royal family fled to Brazil. Work ceased until the reign of Luís I (1861–89) and his Italian bride, Princess Maria Pia of Savoy. They finished building the palace and furnished it with lavish trappings including Gobelins tapestries, oriental ceramics, crystal chandeliers and rare Portuguese furniture. A new contemporary wing houses the Royal Treasure Museum (www.tesouroreal.pt/en; daily 10am–6pm), where you can see Portugal's crown jewels and other valuable treasures, including ornate silver tableware.

MOSTEIRO DOS JERÓNIMOS

Only a short stroll westwards along the Rua de Belém is Lisbon's largest and most impressive religious monument, the **Mosteiro dos Jerónimos** ⑱ (Monastery of the Hieronymites; www.mosteiro jeronimos.gov.pt; Tue–Sun 9.30am–6pm), a UNESCO World Heritage Site. Commissioned by Manuel I with the windfall of riches brought back by Portuguese ships from the East, the monastery is a testament to a confident and faithful nation. The convent wing was destroyed in the 1755 earthquake, but the church and cloister survived, classic examples of 16th-century style.

The vast south façade of the church, parallel to the river, is mostly unadorned limestone, making the few embellishments all the more remarkable. The main portal is a brilliant example of intricately carved stonework, as are the church's tall Manueline columns (this style bridged the gap between the Gothic and Renaissance styles in Portugal). The effect is one of immense height and space.

The first architect in charge was a Frenchman, Diogo Boitac, who was succeeded by the Spaniard Juan de Castillo, responsible for the cloister and main portal.

Inside the church are the royal tombs of Manuel I, his wife Dona Maria, and others, set on pompous sculptured elephants, a tribute to the newly discovered marvels of the East. Near the west door are the modern tombs of two giants of Portugal's Golden Age, Vasco da Gama and the poet Luís de Camões.

Once you leave the church (don't miss the fine sculptural work surrounding the exterior of the main door), turn right and visit the **cloister**, an airy two-level structure of strikingly original proportions and perspectives. Note the clever intersection of both sharp angles and arches. No two columns are the same.

MONASTERY MUSEUMS

The south section of the monastery has been restored and forms a beautiful setting for the **Museu Nacional de Arqueologia** ⑲

Carved stonework outside the Mosteiro dos Jerónimos

(National Museum of Archaeology; www.museuarqueologia.gov.
pt; Tue–Sun 10am–6pm, currently closed and due to reopen in
2025), an important collection of ancient relics, including Stone
Age tools, Bronze Age jewels, Roman sculptures and mosaics, and
some exquisite medieval carving, most breathtaking of which is a
tomb depicting Jesus and St Francis.

Portugal's fascinating maritime heritage is documented at the
Museu da Marinha (Maritime Museum; http://museu.marinha.
pt; daily 10am–5pm, May–Sept until 6pm), which is housed in the
west and northern wings of the monastery and in new buildings
around the square opposite the entrance. Among the museum's
collection are hundreds of models of various ship types through

MANUELINE ARCHITECTURE

The Portuguese may be principally known for *azulejo* designs and
port wine, but equally important is the ornate style of architecture
and stone carving that appeared in Portugal in the late 15th century. It flourished for only a few decades, mostly during the reign of
Manuel I (1495–1521), for which it was christened Manueline.

Probably triggered by the great ocean voyages of discovery, it
took late Gothic as a base and added fanciful decoration, dramatic touches that were frequently references to the sea. Stone was
carved like knotted rope and sculpted into imitation coral, seahors-
es, nets and waves, as well as non-nautical designs. The style first
appeared in the small Igreja de Jesus in Setúbal, Lisbon's Torre de
Belém and the Mosteiro dos Jerónimos. The style reached a peak of
complexity in the unfinished chapels of the monastery at Batalha,
between Lisbon and Coimbra. In the early 16th century, the style
fell out of favour, and by 1540 Portugal had joined the rest of Europe in building in the more sober Renaissance style.

the ages, and numerous artefacts such as naval uniforms, maps and navigation equipment.

Also on display is a delightful sculpture of the archangel Raphael that accompanied Vasco da Gama on his first voyage of exploration in 1497. More recent are the handsome royal suites from the *Amália*, the 1901 royal yacht that belonged to King Carlos I, who was an amateur marine biologist. Pride of place goes

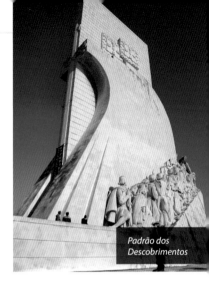

Padrão dos Descobrimentos

to the huge galliot, or brigantine, built in 1785 to celebrate a royal marriage, with seats for 80 oarsmen. The last time it was on the River Tagus was in 1957, carrying Queen Elizabeth II of Britain on a state visit. Next to it is the seaplane piloted by Portuguese aviators that in 1922 made the first flight across the South Atlantic. The museum's educational attractions continue with the **Planetário de Marinha** (www.museu.marinha.pt; Tues–Fri 9.30am–noon & 1.30–4pm, Sat & Sun 10am–noon & 1.30–4.30pm), where you can watch shows about the skies and stars.

BERARDO'S MUSEUM AND THE DISCOVERIES MONUMENT

In the arts hub that is the **Centro Cultural de Belém** (www.ccb. pt), the **Museu Colecção Berardo ⑳** (Berardo Collection Museum; Praça do Império; www.museuberardo.pt; daily 10am–7pm; free on Sat) displays the incredible modern art collection of billionaire

Centro Cultural

Across the road from the Jerónimos Monastery is the Centro Cultural de Belém, built in 1992. It houses the fantastic Museu Colecção Berardo, with a superb collection of modern art, stages temporary exhibitions, and holds concerts in its auditoriums. With shops and cafés, it is well worth visiting to find out what events are taking place.

José Berardo against gleaming white walls, with a roll call of contemporary greats, including Andy Warhol, Paula Rego, Mondrian, Picasso and more.

The arresting **Padrão dos Descobrimentos** ㉑ (Monument to the Discoveries; www.padraodosdescobrimentos.pt; Mar–Sept daily 10am–7pm, Oct–Feb daily 10am–6pm), built in 1960 to commemorate the 500th anniversary of Henry the Navigator's death, juts from the riverbank like a caravel cresting a wave.

On the prow stands Prince Henry, looking out across the river and wearing, as always, his distinctive round hat. The figures behind him represent noted explorers, crusaders, astronomers, cartographers, chroniclers and others instrumental in Portugal's Age of Discovery. A lift followed by stairs leads to the top and a superb view.

TORRE DE BELÉM

Finally, there is the UNESCO World Heritage Site, **Torre de Belém** ㉒ (Tower of Belém; www.torrebelem.pt; Tue–Sun 9.30am–6pm), erected in 1515 to defend the entry to Lisbon. This fortress is one of the finest examples of Manueline architecture, with its battlements, corner turrets and stonework featuring the repeated theme of the Cross. After crossing the wooden bridge, climb several floors to a top-level terrace that looks out over the Tagus.

NORTH LISBON

At the north end of Avenida da Liberdade, beyond the Marquês de Pombal rotunda, is a formal park, **Parque Eduardo VII**, its well-manicured lawns and shrubs flanked by wooded areas and gardens. So thrilled were the Portuguese by a royal visit at the turn of the 20th century that they named the park after Britain's king, Edward VII.

Lisbon's most original botanical triumph occupies the northwest corner of the park. Known as **Estufa Fria ㉓** (the Cold House; Tues–Sun Oct–Mar 9am–5pm, Apr–Sept 10am–7pm), this garden was created in the early 20th century on the site of a quarry, and it owes its name to the fact that its simple wooden lath roof gives shade but no heat, allowing plants from a variety of backgrounds to grow as naturally as possible, pro-tected from the Lisboan extremes of climate. Paths weave their way through the enormous space among species from Africa, Asia and South America. At the far side, a doorway leads through to the cavernous **Estufa Quente** (the Hot House), which was built at the end of the 1950s on the highest point of the quarry. Its roof and walls are made of glass, to capture the max-imum amount of light and heat, so that more tropical species can thrive here.

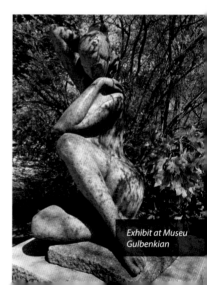

Exhibit at Museu Gulbenkian

MUSEU GULBENKIAN

To the north of Parque Eduardo VII, off Avenida António Augusto Aguiar, is one of the world's great museums, **Museu Gulbenkian** ❷ (Gulbenkian Museum; Avenida da Berna 45; https://gulben kian.pt; Wed–Mon 10am–6pm). It was created to house one of the finest private art collections in Europe, acquired by an Armenian billionaire, Calouste Gulbenkian, and later bequeathed to the Portuguese state. A great philanthropist who died in Lisbon in 1955, Gulbenkian meticulously acquired acclaimed masterpieces and built up an excellent and wide-ranging collection.

Surrounded by its own perfectly planned and maintained 17-acre park, the museum houses a huge collection, which begins chronologically, with Egyptian ceramics and sculptures dating back to around 2700BC, delicate and perfectly preserved. The handsome statue of the judge Bes is inscribed with hieroglyphs that date it from the reign of Pharaoh Psamtik I (7th century BC).

A large section of the museum is devoted to art of the Islamic East, and includes ancient fabrics, costumes and carpets, ceramics, glassware and illuminated pages from the Koran. The survey of Western art begins in the 11th century with illuminated parchment manuscripts. Tiny ivory sculptures of religious scenes come from 14th-century France, and there are a number of well-preserved tapestries from the Flemish and Italian workshops of the 16th century.

Paintings by Dutch and Flemish masters include works by Hals, Van Dyck and Ruysdael. Pride of place is given to two Rembrandts: *Figure of an Old Man* and a painting of a helmeted warrior believed to be Pallas Athene or Alexander the Great, probably modelled by Rembrandt's son Titus.

The impressive hall of Chinese porcelain begins with the Yuan dynasty (13th–14th century; around the time of Marco Polo) and goes on to some exquisite items from the 17th and 18th centuries.

Torre de Belém

Miraculously unmarred by the forces of time, each object is representative of the pinnacle of a particular school of art.

The last room of the museum contains 169 items by Gulbenkian's friend René Lalique (1860–1945), the talented and versatile French jeweller. On display are exquisite Art Nouveau combs, pendants, bracelets and necklaces, including a dazzling, bejewelled brooch of nine entwined serpents.

The **Centro de Arte Moderna** ㉕ (Modern Art Centre; as above; currently closed for renovation) is also a part of the Gulbenkian Foundation. Its collection includes the best 20th-century Portuguese art, with some excellent works by Amadeo de Souza Cardoso, Vieira da Silva and Almada Negreiros, particularly of society types and Lisbon café life. There are also a couple of early Paula Rego abstracts, from 1935, as well as works by British artists such as David Hockney and Henry Moore.

The Foundation has exhibition spaces and concert halls where musical performances and ballets take place. There is also a library, with occasional free Sunday lunchtime concerts, a bookshop and a restaurant.

AQUEDUTO DAS ÁGUAS LIVRES

A landmark that is most often seen by those heading out of town is the soaring arches of **Aqueduto das Águas Livres** ㉖ (a freshwater aqueduct), which spans an impressive 18km (11 miles) across the Alcântara valley north of downtown Lisbon. Fresh water was first carried across the aqueduct in 1748 and, since it managed to survive the earthquake, it continues to flow. It is possible to walk across a 1.5km section of the aqueduct, though you'll need a head for heights. The walkable section is accessed off a quiet residential street through a small park in Campolide, 1km north of Praça das Amoreiras.

CALOUSTE GULBENKIAN

At the dawn of the Oil Age, a far-sighted Turkish-born Armenian put up money to help finance drilling in Mesopotamia (now Iraq), then part of the Turkish Empire. For his part, he received 5 percent of the Iraq Petroleum Company. Two world wars and the fuelling of millions of cars, planes and ships made Calouste Gulbenkian rich beyond imagination. He became a knowledgeable and dedicated collector of antiquities and great art, beginning with Turkish and Persian carpets, Armenian and Arabic manuscripts, and Greek and Roman coins. His passions spread to include ancient Egyptian art, Chinese porcelain and Western painting. His mission was acquiring perfect examples in each of his chosen fields.

Gulbenkian (who had British nationality for much of his life) was preparing to travel to the United States when he fell ill in Lisbon. He was so impressed with his treatment here that he decided to stay, establishing a philanthropic foundation to which he left most of his money and his collections when he died in 1955. The Gulbenkian Museum is his centrepiece, complemented by several other cultural facilities in Portugal, including the Modern Art Centre, regional museums, a planetarium and educational institutes.

Along with the motorway to Cascais, the aqueduct slices through the city's biggest park, **Monsanto**. Eucalyptus, cypress, cedar, umbrella pines and oak trees all thrive on the rolling hillsides and there are some impressive *miradouros*, giving outstanding views over Lisbon and the estuary. Apart from calm and fresh air, the park contains leisure and sports grounds, bars and restaurants, plus a municipal camping ground.

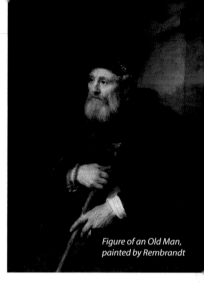

Figure of an Old Man, painted by Rembrandt

PARQUE DAS NAÇÕES

Lisbon, and the whole of Portugal, pinned much hope on the city's hosting of the World Expo in 1998. Celebrating the 'Heritage of the Oceans', it was an opportunity for the nation to pay tribute to its former maritime greatness and reintroduce itself to the world.

Lisbon used the occasion to reinvigorate a run-down industrial area east of the city, creating a high-tech entertainment park, along with new shopping and nightlife areas. Framing the park is the futuristic railway station, **Estação do Oriente**, designed by the Spanish architect Santiago Calatrava as a major terminal for destinations around the country, a pristine shopping mall and the sleek Ponte Vasco da Gama (Vasco da Gama Bridge) extending across the Tagus into the horizon – Europe's longest bridge at 17.2km (10.75 miles).

The **Parque das Nações** (Nations' Park; www.portaldasnacoes. pt) complex extends 5km (3 miles) along the riverfront, principally drawing visitors to its world-class aquarium, which served as the Oceans Pavilion during the Expo, and has since become one of the city's primary attractions.

The complex won the award for best urban development in Iberia in 1999. Designed by the American Peter Chermayeff, the **Oceanário de Lisboa** ㉗ (www.oceanario.pt; daily 10am–7pm, summer until 8pm), resembling a marooned oil derrick or space station from the set of a sci-fi thriller, is one of the largest and finest aquariums in the world. Reached by a footbridge, it houses large tanks representing four distinct marine ecosystems – Antarctic, Indian, Pacific and Atlantic – with more than 10,000 examples of marine life in 200 species, taken from across the world. You'll see penguins in the

Futuristic architecture at Parque das Nações

Antarctic section and otters in the Pacific. As visitors make their way around the massive circular aquarium, the size of four Olympic-size swimming pools, tiger sharks, manta rays and schools of brightly coloured fish glide silently by, overhead and beneath the observation decks.

Park panorama

A high point of the Parque das Nações is the 145m (475ft) Torre Vasco da Gama – the tallest structure in Portugal – with a Michelin-starred restaurant at the top that looks out to the Atlantic and back down the river at Lisbon.

Parque das Nações is a good place for families. There are whimsical fountains, paddle boats, garden playgrounds, bowling lanes and an aerial cable car running the length of the waterfront.

The **Pavilhão do Conhecimento** (the Pavilion of Knowledge; www.pavconhecimento.pt; Tue–Fri 10am–6pm, Sat–Sun 11am–7pm), is a thrilling, highly-educational, hands-on museum of science and technology.

Sporting events, such as basketball and tennis, and concerts by big-name international and local performers, are held at the mushroom-like **Atlântico Hall** arena (Altice Arena), which functioned as the Utopia Pavilion during the Expo. The **Teatro Camões** is home to the excellent national ballet company (www.cnb.pt).

Many restaurants and bars have moved into the marina area, transforming it into an animated nightspot, and the construction of hotels and residential housing are creating a desirable suburb. The mall around the Metro station attracts late-night and Sunday shoppers.

Among the former pavilions notable for their architectural interest is the **Portugal Pavilion** beside the marina, by the Pritzker prize-winning Portuguese architect Álvaro Siza Vieira. The pavilion has an astonishing curved and suspended roof 67m (221ft) long and weighing 1,400 tonnes.

ACROSS THE TAGUS

With a span of 2.3km (1.5 miles), the **Ponte 25 de Abril** ㉘ across the River Tagus became the longest suspension bridge in Europe when it was opened in 1966. Originally named in honour of the nation's dictator, after the revolution of 1974 the name 'Salazar' was removed, and for quite a time it was known simply as 'the bridge'. In an about-face, it was renamed after the date of the Carnation Revolution. Though its bold red colour is quite striking, the bridge lacks the grace of the Golden Gate Bridge in San Francisco, with which it is often compared.

Just across the river, above Cacilhas and looming up over the bridge's tollbooths, is Lisbon's take on Rio de Janeiro's landmark, the enormous **statue of Cristo Rei** (Christ the King), built in 1959. Almost 30m (100ft) tall, it stands on a pedestal that is another 82m (269ft) high.

A chapel, the Santuário de Cristo Rei (https://cristorei.pt; daily 10am–6pm), is housed in the base of the towering monument, where there is also a cafeteria. Take the lift up to the viewing terrace at the top of the pedestal for a glorious 360-degree panoramic view of the estuary, the bridge, all of Lisbon and a vast expanse of Portugal to the south, including the Serra da Arrábida (see page 79).

In Cacilhas docks, not far from the ferry terminal, the **Fragata D. Fernando II e Glória** is berthed (Tue–Sun 10am–5pm, May–Sept until 6pm; http://ccm.marinha.pt/pt/dfernando). You can look round this beautiful vessel, the Portuguese navy's last sailing ship, which was built

Reaching Cristo Rei

To visit the statue of Cristo Rei you can drive across the bridge or take one of the orange ferries from Cais do Sodré to Cacilhas and then a taxi or a bus marked 'Cristo Rei'.

Cycling by Ponte 25 de Abril

in the Indian colony of Damão in 1843. There's also a chance to board the submarine that sits near the frigate.

EXCURSIONS FROM LISBON

One of the great attractions of Lisbon is the fact that a number of desirable excursions are only a very short distance from the capital – there are highlights west, south and north of the city. Whether you're looking for grand palaces, beach resorts, awe-inspiring abbeys or a charming romantic town lodged in the mountains, there's plenty to explore in the environs.

QUELUZ

An easy half-day outing is to **Palácio Nacional de Queluz** ㉙ (www.parquesdesintra.pt; daily 9am–6pm), 14km (9 miles) west of Lisbon. To reach it, take a bus tour or a commuter train from Rossio

station to Queluz-Belas. By car it's 20 minutes on the motorway through the forest of Monsanto; the turn-off on the way to Sintra is clearly signposted. You're hardly out of Lisbon's mushrooming suburbs before you're alongside the elegant palace.

Pedro III commissioned this sumptuous, pretty pink summer palace, which was built in the second half of the 18th century by the Frenchman Jean-Baptiste Robillon and the Portuguese Mateus Vicente de Oliveira. As a working official residence for the royal family, Queluz thrived mostly during the reign of Maria I (1777–99), Pedro III's wife. The queen suffered from bouts of depression, which deepened into madness, and visitors to the palace told of her shrieking fits.

From the road, the palace seems relatively unprepossessing, but inside, Portuguese modesty is totally abandoned, and Queluz is a model of only slightly tattered splendour. Though the palace lost much to French invasions (it was used by General

Andoche Junot as his headquarters during the Peninsular War) and a 1934 fire, it manages to preserve an air of 18th-century royal privilege. The **throne room** is one of the most lavish, with overpowering chandeliers and walls and ceilings layered with gilt. The **Sala dos Embaixadores** (Hall of Ambassadors) has a floor like a huge chessboard in addition to a wealth of mirrors and a *trompe l'oeil* ceiling.

The **Palace Gardens** are the pride of Queluz and seem never-ending, with clipped hedges in perfect geometric array, bushes barbered into inventive shapes, imaginative fountains and armies of statues. The huge old magnolia trees and orange trees close by relieve some of the formality. Royal guests once entered the garden via the pompous but original **Escadaria dos Leões** (Lions' Staircase).

In the early 19th century dozens of live animals – not just dogs, but lions and wolves – were boarded at Queluz, which was then the site of the royal zoo.

One rather original attraction is the man-made river. Enclosed between retaining walls covered in precious *azulejos*, a real stream was diverted to pass through the huge palace grounds, and was dammed so that the level of the water could be raised whenever the royal residents wanted to go for a boat ride.

The former royal kitchen has been converted into a prestigious restaurant run by the *pousada* hotel chain (www.pousadas.pt/uk/hotel/pousada-queluz/dining?restId=21). With giant

By train to Sintra

The easiest way to reach Sintra is by train. It's also accessible by car, but the roads can get very busy, and parking is difficult. However, a car is useful for access to some of the outlying sights, such as the Montserrate Gardens, or to reach the coast.

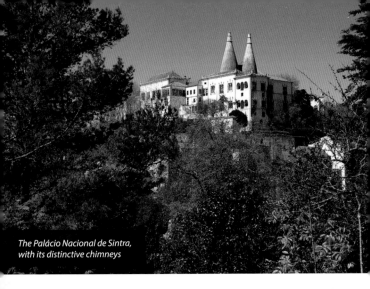

The Palácio Nacional de Sintra, with its distinctive chimneys

old utensils, a fireplace big enough for a crowd to walk into, and lots of atmosphere, the place is called – understandably – *Cozinha Velha*, or 'Old Kitchen'.

SINTRA

Sintra ③⓪ is a magical, palace-dotted landscape, which feels like it has sprung from a storybook. Easily reached by train from Rossio, and nestled into the Serra de Sintra, 25km (16 miles) northwest of Lisbon, it was once a coveted summer retreat for royals; today it's a romantic getaway for people from all over the world. Clustered throughout the forested hillsides are old palaces and estates with spectacular vistas. Two peaks in the range are crowned by reminders of Sintra's illustrious past: Castelo dos Mouros, the ruins of a castle built by occupying Moors in the 8th century, and Palácio de Pena, the multicoloured fantasy palace built by a German noble-man for his Portuguese wife. The views from either of these points extends as far as the sea, and the entire area, thick with vegetation and paths through the hills, provides spectacular trekking.

Right in the centre of town is the **Palácio Nacional de Sintra** (also called the *Paço Real*, or Royal Palace; www.parquesdesintra. pt; daily 9.30am–6pm). Except for its two huge, white conical chimneys, from the outside it looks like a fairly ordinary hulk of a palace. Its real treasures lie inside.

A summer home for Portuguese kings since the early 14th century, the palace's design became more and more unpredictable and haphazard as wings were added over the centuries, with back-to-back medieval and Manueline styles. The resulting interiors and furnishings are remarkable, including some of the oldest and most valuable *azulejos* in Portugal, which line many of the rooms.

Every room in the Palácio Nacional has a story to tell. During the 17th century, the dull-witted Afonso VI was pressured into abdicating for the benefit of the country, therefore allowing his more effective brother, Pedro II, to become king.

When a plot to restore Afonso to the throne was discovered, the former monarch was exiled to Sintra. For nine years, until he died in 1683, he was imprisoned in a simple room of the Palácio Nacional. It's said that the worn floor is a result of Afonso's constant pacing up and down.

Sala dos Cisnes

A large ground-floor hall, **Sala das Pegas** (Magpie Salon), tells a very different story. João I (1385–1433) was caught by Queen Philippa kissing one of her ladies-in-waiting. The palace gossips had a field day until the king ordered the entire ceiling of the hall closed and painted with magpies, as many as there were ladies-in-waiting, 136 in fact. Each held in its beak a ribbon with the king's motto, *por bem* (in honour). The royal rebuke, the king's way of saying 'so what' and 'shut up', had the desired effect.

The so-called **Sala dos Cisnes** (Swan Room) is decorated with ceiling panels painted with swans, each in a different position. There are also ceilings with intricate designs in the *mudéjar* style influenced by Moorish art.

The palace's landmark twin chimneys, shaped like inverted cones, were used to let the smoke out of the massive kitchen when oxen were being roasted for large banquets given for visiting dignitaries.

Moors' castle and the Pena Palace

A special bus climbs a steep road with hairpin turns into the *serra* from Sintra to visit some spectacular monuments. The oldest, **Castelo dos Mouros** (Moors' Castle; www.parquesdesintra.pt;

SINTRA'S COUNTRY MARKET

On the second and last Sunday of each month, a country fair is held in São Pedro do Sintra, a village adjacent to Sintra – be prepared to encounter traffic jams. The origins of the fair go back to the 12th century. In the open market you can buy home-made bread, cheese, sausages and snacks such as churros. Antiques collectors will find many possibilities here, from religious statues, rustic furniture and rugs, to arts and crafts and domestic bric-a-brac.

The fantastical Palácio da Pena

daily 10am–6pm), hugs a rocky ridge overlooking the town. It was erected during the 8th century, soon after the Moors occupied Portugal. The dauntless Dom Afonso Henriques conquered it for the Christians in 1147, a major victory in the reconquest of Portugal.

Today the castle is a ruin, but a fascinating one, its crenellated walls still severe. Those with the energy to do so should climb the ramparts to the top for incredible views of the entire forested area, to the sea beyond, and across the treetops to Sintra's most famous monument, the Palácio da Pena. It's easy to pick out individual *quintas* (estates) in their privileged seclusion.

Further up the same winding road on the hilltop, the **Palácio da Pena** (www.parquesdesintra.pt; daily 10am–6pm; the park stays open til 7pm), more than 450m (1,500ft) above sea-level, is an outrageous Victorian folly reached by way of a park so lush with flowering trees and vines it resembles a tropical rainforest. In

1511, Manuel I had a monastery built on this site. It was mostly destroyed in the earthquake of 1755, though a notable chapel and cloister survive. The present building is a bizarre and extravagant cocktail of Gothic, Renaissance, Manueline and Moorish architecture, fashioned as a love nest for Maria II (1834–53) and her smitten husband, Ferdinand of Saxe-Coburg-Gotha. Few have had the wealth to indulge their free-running fantasies so grandly. Like a child's dream castle, the exterior is a wild, layered construction painted pink, yellow, grey and red, with crenellated turrets, a studded archway and monsters guarding doorways. Inside, rooms are full of imaginative, ornate and, in some cases, suffocatingly sumptuous details. The views from the Disney-esque terraces of the platforms sweep all the way from the Atlantic to Lisbon.

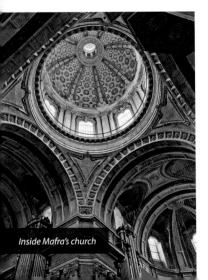
Inside Mafra's church

AROUND SINTRA

Located in and around Sintra are: the **Quinta da Regaleira**, a fantastic late 19th-century turreted mansion, with magical gardens speckled with follies such as the 'initiation well', which you can walk into down a spiralling staircase; the **Montserrate Palace Gardens**, wild, lush, and ideal for hiking; the **Palácio de Seteais**, an 18th-century palace that today is Sintra's fanciest hotel, and Sintra's excellent **Museum of Modern Art**.

The beach at Ericeira

A short hop from Sintra are the attractive village of **Colares** and the beach at **Praia das Maçãs**. Sintra's helpful tourist information office, on Praça da República in the old quarter, can direct you to any of these.

MAFRA AND ERICEIRA

The **Palácio Nacional de Mafra** ㉛ (www.palaciomafra.gov.pt; Wed–Mon 9.30am–5.30pm) at Mafra, is 40km (25 miles) to the northwest of Lisbon, and can be reached by bus from the terminal outside Campo Grande Metro station. In modest Portugal, the dimensions of this convent and palace are quite staggering. The frontage of the building, often likened to Spain's Escorial, measures over 220m (726ft). Mafra is so enormous that it is clearly visible from Sintra, approximately 16km (10 miles) away.

This monumental extravagance is attributable to João V, who in 1711 conceived this project to celebrate the long-awaited birth of his first child, Princess Dona Maria, after three years of marriage. A few statistics show the colossal scale of the project: 5,200 doorways, 2,500 windows and a 50,000-strong army of artists, artisans and labourers. A single carillon of 50 bells cost a shipload of gold. 'So cheap?' the king is said to have exclaimed. 'I'll take two.'

Your visit to the monastery-palace will take you from the apartments of João V at one end of the structure to the queen's apartments at the other end. The convent **library** is the undisputed highlight; it has a vaulted ceiling, a precious wood floor and tall shelves housing 30,000 books, making it the largest one-room library in Portugal. The **hospital** is a church with 16 private sickrooms lining the nave, so that patients could hear mass from their beds.

At Mafra is the church of Santo André, where Pedro Hispano was a priest before becoming Pope John XI in 1276, He remains Portugal's only pope.

Another 10km (6 miles) towards the coast is the fishing village and growing resort of **Ericeira** 🕙, now a popular surfing destination. The old section is a winsome town of cobbled streets winding between whitewashed cottages, with everything clean, neat and treasured by inhabitants and visitors alike. Ericeira received its town charter around 750 years ago, but scarcely attracted any attention until 1910, when Portugal's last king, Manuel II, hastily arrived from Mafra, and in its little port, boarded the royal yacht with his family to sail off into exile.

ESTORIL COAST

The Costa do Estoril (formerly called Costa do Sol) begins just west of Lisbon and goes all the way around the tip of the peninsula to Guincho on the open Atlantic. Those seeking pollution-free swimming (see page 91) usually head for Guincho, but the famous old resort of **Estoril** 🚯 itself, some 24km (15 miles) from Lisbon, is still worth a visit.

The half-hour train journey from Cais do Sodré station in Lisbon to Estoril goes through former fishing villages now turned into soulless commuter suburbs. If you go by the motorway (toll road) you will see nothing of them at all, but the coastal road still provides a scenic drive.

The railway station at Estoril is right alongside the beach. On the other side of the tracks (and across the coast road) is a formal park, the front lawn of the town's glitzy casino. With its nightclub, restaurants, bars, cinema, live music, shops and gaming rooms, this is Estoril's one-stop, after-dark amusement centre. In spite of the modern decor, the casino maintains an old-fashioned pace. Gambling is suspended only two nights a year: Good Friday and

On the seafront at Cascais

Christmas Eve. Legend has it that somebody broke the bank one Good Friday, prompting a superstitious management to declare it a holiday thenceforth. (Officials dismiss the story as wishful thinking.)

The rest of Estoril is a mix of standard high-rise tourist hotels, Victorian villas and sleek contemporary mansions tucked away behind green curtains of palms, eucalyptus, pines and vines. In the first half of the 20th century, dignitaries and monarchs, either unexpectedly unemployed or exiled, gravitated to Estoril or Cascais and luxurious hideaways.

As early as the mid-18th century, Estoril was attracting visitors because of its warm climate and thermal spa baths, which were considered good for liver complaints. It was a hangout for exiles and spies taking advantage of Portugal's neutrality during World

Surfer in Guincho

War II, and Ian Fleming was inspired to write *Casino Royale* after his stay here. Long before that, however, prehistoric settlers had dug cave-cemeteries out of the limestone near the beach, discovered in 1944.

Cascais

Nearby **Cascais** ㉞, which sits on a pretty curved bay, is a highly attractive former fishing village, now a popular tourist resort. It's liveliest round Largo Luís de Camões, at one end of Rua Frederico Arouca, the main mosaic-paved pedestrian thoroughfare.

Cascais' main square is charming, with swirling-patterned monochrome paving underfoot. The **Paços do Concelho** (Town Hall) has stately windows with iron railings, separated by panels of *azulejos* depicting saints. The fire station occupies a place of honour between the town hall and an attractive church, while in the square itself, stands a statue of Pedro I.

The sturdy-looking 17th-century fort, the **Cidadela** (Citadel), is one of the few buildings to have survived the earthquake and tidal wave of 1755. Originally a sea fort and then a summer retreat for Portuguese royalty, the Citadela is still used by the Portuguese president to entertain his guests. A chapel within the walls contains an image of St Anthony, traditionally carried on the back of a white mule in the parade on the feast day of Santo António (13 June).

After an overdose of sun and salt, the municipal park down the road is a cool relief. The palace in this park is a lovely villa housing the **Museu dos Condes de Castro Guimarães** (Museum of the Counts of Castro Guimarães; Rua Júlio Pereira de Mello; https://bairrodosmuseus.cascais.pt/list/museu/museu-condes-de-castro-guimaraes; Tue–Sun 10am–6pm), a museum with archaeological remains, artworks, old furniture, gold and silver. For a more complete picture of the resort's fishing heritage and

The main square of Cascais

royal connections, visit the intriguing **Museu do Mar – Rei Dom Carlos** (King Carlos Museum of the Seas; https://bairrodosmuseus.cascais.pt/list/museu/museu-do-mar-rei-d-carlos; Tue–Sun 10am–6pm), which has historic photographs of the king, who was an enthusiastic marine biologist, at leisure, as well as the costumes and customs of the fisherfolk.

Highlight of the Cascais museums, however, is the **Casa das Histórias** (https://casadashistoriaspaularego.com; Tue–Sun 10am–6pm), dedicated to the artist, Paula Rego (1935–2022), who grew up in the town. With its distinctive ochre towers, the airy museum was designed by the famous architect Eduardo Souto de Moura, and puts on exhibitions of Rego's disturbing but beautiful collages, drawings and paintings, as well as those by her late English husband Victor Willing.

The road out of Cascais to the west passes **Boca do Inferno** (Mouth of Hell), a geological curiosity where, in rough weather, the waves send up astonishingly high spouts of spray accompanied by ferocious sound effects. On a day when the sea is calm, you'll wonder what all the fuss is about.

Cabo da Roca

At **Guincho**, you have the choice of either a sandy beach or the rocks to fish from, but be careful – they face the open sea and it's often rough, and hence a windsurfer's heaven. Just up the coast you can see the windswept cape of **Cabo da Roca,** the most westerly point of mainland Europe. You can reach the cape by continuing on from Guincho, through Malveira, and then turning left. A right turn at the same points leads you along a winding road through the glorious, pine-scented **Serra de Sintra**, finishing up back in Sintra (see page 66).

SOUTH OF LISBON

Sesimbra

It's around 32km (20 miles) south from Lisbon over the bridge to the calm, clean seashore at **Sesimbra** ㉟. The beach is the main draw for the mostly Portuguese crowd that gathers here at

Busy beach at Sesimbra

weekends and holidays, not least for its splendid seafood restaurants. Narrow but long, the beach is sheltered from the brunt of the Atlantic tides and harsh winds. Sesimbra was an important fishing centre, and you can still see fishing boats setting out from the **harbour** at the far, western end of the town, to bring home their catches of sardines and mackerel.

Largo 5 de Outubro is a small square in the centre of town, where locals sit and gossip under a giant floral canopy of bougainvillea. Adjacent is the **Misericórdia Church**, with its upturned keel roof. Founded during the 15th century, it contains the much-venerated image of Senhor Jesus das Chagas, the patron of the Sesimbra fishing community, and a painting of Nossa Senhora da Misericórdia.

The **castle walls** silhouetted on the hilltop above Sesimbra are the genuine article, though restored. During the Middle Ages the whole town was up there, protected against sea raiders by the walls and the altitude. The Moors built the enclave, lost it to Dom Afonso Henriques in 1165, and won it back again for a few years before having to move out permanently in 1200. Within the outer fortifications is the Church of Our Lady of the Consolation of the Castle, destroyed during the 12th century and rebuilt during the 18th. Take a peek inside: the walls are covered with *azulejos* from floor to ceiling. The castle is

Boca do Inferno

open daily and free to visitors. The view down to the curve of the coast and back to the Arrábida mountains is magnificent.

Serra da Arrábida

The topographical highlight of the Arrábida peninsula is the **Serra da Arrábida**, a mountain chain approximately 35km (22 miles) long that protects the coast from the strong north winds and accounts for the Mediterranean vegetation. In the west the peninsula ends with the dramatic cliffs of **Cabo Espichel**.

The 12km (7.5-mile) route across the Serra is winding and narrow, but it provides an attractive introduction to the wonderfully rugged **Parque Natural da Arrábida ㉞**, which covers more than 10,000 hectares (24,700 acres) and rises a sheer 500m (1,650ft) from the sea.

Wild slopes contrast with the intense blue of the sea below; come in spring and the park is bright with wild flowers. Built

Fresh catch on the coast

in the sixteenth century by Franciscan monks, the white buildings of the Convento **da Arrábida** tumble down a steep hillside offering stunning ocean views. Down below, on the coast, the little beach spot of **Portinho da Arrábida** is popular with Portuguese weekenders.

Setúbal

Setúbal ㉟, the district capital, is a 45-minute drive from Lisbon by motorway, longer if you take the picturesque route via Sesimbra and Arrábida. (There are also direct buses and trains from Lisbon.) This is olive and citrus country, with cows grazing among the trees. The further south you go, the more significant the vineyards; the Setúbal region produces a highly regarded Muscatel.

Setúbal is a conglomeration of market town, industrial centre and resort, and is Portugal's third-largest fishing port. Narrow, cobbled shopping streets twist through the centre of the city. Some action is usually taking place down in the fishing harbour when boats of all sizes return with their freshly caught fish.

Setúbal's greatest historical and artistic treasure, the Gothic **Igreja de Jesus** (June to mid-Sept Tue–Sat 10am–5pm, Sun 3–7pm; mid-Sept to May Tue–Sat 10am–5pm, Sun 2–5pm), was built around 1490 by the great French architect Diogo Boitac, who later built Lisbon's glorious Jerónimos Monastery (see page 50).

The adjoining monastery has been converted into the **Museu de Cidade** (Tue–Sat 10am–6pm, Sun summer 3–7pm, winter

2–6pm) with a mixture of early Portuguese paintings, including a series of the life of Jesus, archaeological odds and ends, antique furniture and tiles. The cloister was reconstructed after the 1755 earthquake, but since then excavation has revealed parts of the original patio.

The **Galeria Municipal do Banco de Portugal** (Tue–Fri 11am–2pm and 3–6pm, Sat 11am–1pm and 2–6pm, Sun 2–6pm) is housed in a beautiful Art Nouveau former bank and hosts exhibitions and events. A permanent exhibition dedicated to the Portuguese Romantic poet Manuel Maria Barbosa du Bocage, who was born in Setúbal, can be seen at **Casa Bocage house museum** (Tue–Fri 9am–noon & 12.30pm–2pm, Sat 2–6pm).

The 16th-century star-shaped fort, high above the town to the west, has great views (Tue–Sun 10am–6pm; see page 141).

Barrels stored at a winery in Setúbal

Easter procession

THINGS TO DO

SHOPPING

Many of Lisbon's shops seem not to have changed in style for at least 100 years, and have an appealing old-fashioned aesthetic, while in the narrow streets of Bairro Alto, young designers show off their latest creations with DJs playing while you browse. In many places you can buy handicrafts, notably ceramics, which have been produced in the same way for hundreds of years. There are also chic boutiques, glittering malls and a wonderfully scruffy outdoor market.

BEST BUYS

Handicrafts excel in Portugal. **Azulejos**, the hand-painted ceramic tiles that have been decorating Portugal's walls throughout the centuries, are one of the top crafts. You can buy a scene on a single blue-and-white tile, an address plaque for your house or a batch to assemble into a picture when you get home. Some shops will paint tiles to order if you have a particular design in mind, and some will copy a photograph.

Delicate Portuguese **embroidery** and **lacework**, especially samples by women on the island of Madeira, is excellent. Hand-embroidered goods, such as tablecloths, napkins and hand towels, also come from the Azores and some mainland towns, notably Viana do Castelo.

Filigree work is of very high quality. Look for silver filigree earrings and delicate brooches, often in the form of flowers or butterflies. Portuguese **pottery** and **ceramics** are found in many designs and colours, from fine porcelain **Vista Alegre** to folksy earthenware. Hand-painted brightly coloured **cockerels** from Barcelos are the ubiquitous national symbol.

Arraiolos, an Alentejo village, has been making fine **wool rugs** in bright colours and graceful designs for centuries. **Hand-woven baskets**, which differ by region, are strong, utilitarian and often pretty. Artefacts made from **cork** are typical; Portugal is the world's leading producer, not only for wine bottles, but also for purses and bags.

Portugal has long been famous for its fortified **port wine** from the Douro Valley near Oporto in the north. Best known as an after-dinner tradition, it also comes in aperitif versions (see page 104). Vintage port from the most select years is what connoisseurs and collectors seek, but there are more accessible ports to take home. Look for aged tawny, LBV (late bottle vintages) or, for something a little more unusual, a bottle of white port.

Madeira wine, from the volcanic soil of the Portuguese island in the Atlantic, is served either before dinner or afterwards as a dessert wine. While these regional wines get much of the attention, Portugal also produces a number of excellent red and white table wines. Look for those from Dão and Alentejo, as well as *vinhos verdes* (young wines) from the Minho.

Hand-painted cockerels

To enjoy the sounds of Portugal back home, take home a classic **fado recording**, perhaps by the late Amália Rodrigues or by Carlos Paredes.

A number of **high-fashion designers** from Portugal – such as Ana Salazar and Fátima Lopes – have gained international attention, and Chiado and Bairro Alto are good places to seek them out. Hand-knitted pullovers in sophisticated designs or chunky fishermen's sweaters from Nazaré are good buys.

The Portuguese leather industry is known throughout the world and jackets, belts, bags, wallets and shoes are popular and good-value buys.

Haberdasher's facade in Baixa

WHERE TO SHOP

Most city shops are open Monday to Friday from 9 or 10am to 7pm (smaller ones might take a lunch break, usually between 1 and 3pm); the more traditional shops close on Saturday at 1pm. Modern shopping malls are usually open from 10am to midnight or later, and sometimes on Sunday.

The **Chiado** district is the place to go for books, smart designer wear and interior design, especially the **Armazéns do Chiado** mall (www.armazensdochiado.com) and Rua Garrett. The French-owned Fnac department store here is popular.

The central grid of streets around Rua Augusta in the **Baixa** contains some wonderfully atmospheric shops, dotted in among the international brands. Traditional foodstuffs, clothing and jewellery are all sold here.

Local produce in Mercado da Ribeira

Across the street from Cais de Sodre station is the renovated, 19th-century **Mercado da Ribeira**, which houses a daily food market (6am–2pm), selling everything from fish, meat and vegetables to formal flower arrangements. It's also home to the Time Out Market (Sun–Thurs 10am–midnight; Fri & Sat 10am–1am), a foodies' paradise with dozens of food stalls representing the best restaurants in Lisbon. Tasting menus are great value and the place has already become one of the favourite meeting points for locals and tourists alike. Markets are fun for their ambience as much as the goods on offer. Behind São Vicente de Fora church, in the Campo de Santa Clara, the **Feira da Ladra** ('Thieves' Market') is held on Tuesday and Saturday from 9am to 3pm. On the fringes of the kitchenware and clothing stalls are dusty treasures and an incredible range of second-hand items.

Lisbon has two main shopping centres. **Amoreiras** (Avenida Engenheiro Duarte Pacheco; www.amoreiras.com) is a pastel-coloured complex laid out over three floors. It houses banks, a post office, cinemas, a health club, supermarkets, a chapel, art galleries, eating places and over 200 shops selling goods from furniture and linen to music, books, china and chocolate. **Centro Columbo** (Avenida Lusiada, Benfica; www.colombo.pt) is the city's largest shopping centre, more akin to a massive leisure complex than a mere shopping mall. Come here for all the major chains, plus cinemas and restaurants. Alternatively, head for the largest branch of the Spanish chain **El Corte Ingles** (Avenida Antonio Augusto Aguiar, 31; www.elcorteingles.pt) or **Atrium Saldanha** (Praça Duque de Saldanha; www.atriumsaldanha.pt), with a great variety of shops and restaurants for snack and light meal options.

Out near Cascais, beside the motorway, **CascaiShopping** (www.cascaishopping.pt) is another shopping complex. For easy shopping closer to town, you might like to try the **Centro Commercial de Alvalade** (www.ccalvalade.pt) and the fashionable but generally expensive **Avenida da Roma**.

ENTERTAINMENT

The Portuguese capital is a great place to party, with venues ranging from *fado* speakeasies to superclubs, and from African nightclubs to alternative bars, clustered in various areas around the city.

Nightclubs, bars and live music. The classic night-time outing in Lisbon is still to the ***fado*** houses in Alfama or Bairro Alto. A century ago, 'respectable' people were reluctant to be seen in a *fado* club; nowadays the danger is not to your reputation, only to your wallet, as tickets and drinks are quite expensive. Many offer dinner as well as drinks.

Good *fado* clubs include Senhor Vinho (Rua do Meio à Lapa 18; tel: 213-972 681; www.srvinho.com), Alfama's A Baiuca (Rua de São Miguel 20; tel: 939-457 098), a low-key local place, and Fado in

Chiado (Espaço Chiado, Rua da Misericordia 14; tel: 961 717 778; www.fadoinchiado.com).

Nightlife areas are clustered around dock areas, and these venues tend towards a more mainstream crowd, but the biggest buzz is to be found in Bairro Alto, where there are nightclubs, jazz clubs and bars for all tastes, some open until 5am.

Eclectic bars include gay-friendly Portas Largas (Rua da Atalaia 105) and Alface Hall (Rua da Norte 96), which has regular live music. North of Bairro Alto, the area around Principe Real is the centre of the city's gay scene and also home to the fantastical bar, Pavilhão Chinês (Rua Dom Pedro V 89-91), worth a visit for a cocktail amid its extraordinary crazy-attic, clutter-lined decor.

The club to visit in Lisbon is riverside Lux (Armazém A, Cais da Pedra a Santa Apolónia; www.luxfragil.com), which is run by nightlife guru Marcel Reis. It's enduringly chic, edgy and interesting, despite being a super-club.

FADO

Fado, the soulful Portuguese song – literally 'fate', translated into music – is based on a story or poem and accompanied by a 12-string guitar. The dramatic atmosphere of a *fado* house adds to the occasion. Guitarists start off the proceedings with a warm-up number. The lights dim, the audience goes quiet, and a spotlight picks out a woman in black who begins to wail out a song of tragedy and despair. Her sultry voice sums up that most Portuguese emotion, *saudade* – a swell of longing, regret and nostalgia. Though most often characterised by melancholy or despair, there are also joyful and relatively upbeat *fados*.

Most *fado* singers are women, but you are also likely to hear a man perform the same sort of ballad with a strong, husky voice.

Fado performers

Concerts and dance. Lisbon's cultural scene offers occasional opera, symphony concerts, ballet and recitals, usually held in winter. The city's opera company is well regarded, and the Gulbenkian Foundation (see page 56) maintains its own symphony orchestra and choir company.

Portugal has three other important symphony orchestras and a national dance company.

Venues include: Coliseu dos Recreios (Rua das Portas de Santo Antão 96; tel: 213-240 580, www.coliseulisboa.com), the second-largest music and events hall in Lisbon; Altice Arena (Parque das Nações; tel: 218-918 409, http://arena.altice.pt), the place for big-time rock bands and Brazilian acts; Museu Gulbenkian (Avenida de Berna 45; tel: 217-823 000, www.gulbenkian.pt), which hosts varied recitals, classical music and dance programmes, including open-air concerts in summer; Teatro Nacional de São Carlos (Rua Serpa Pinto 9; tel: 213-253 000, http://tnsc.pt), Lisbon's opera house; and Centro Cultural de Belém (Praça do Império; tel: 213-612 400, www.ccb.pt), which has a wide programme of cultural performances.

Theatre and cinema. Most of Lisbon's stage plays are comedies and revues – in Portuguese, of course. The best-known theatre is **Teatro Nacional de Dona Maria II** (Praça de Dom Pedro IV, Rossio; tel: 213-250 800, www.tndm.pt).

Cinemas tend to show foreign films in the original language with Portuguese subtitles. **São Jorge** (Avenida Liberdade 175; tel: 213-103 400, www.cinemasaojorge.pt) is a pleasantly renovated cinema with three screens, and often hosts festivals.

Gambling. The **Estoril Casino** (tel: 214-667 700, www.casino-estoril.pt; see page 73) is the big draw for gamblers. To enter the gaming rooms you have to pay a fee and show your passport. The casino is open daily 3pm–3am (closed Christmas Eve). A sign suggests that gentlemen wear jackets after 8pm, but no rules are enforced.

SPORTS

From swimming and hiking to deep-sea fishing, sports enthusiasts have plenty of options in the Lisbon area. The temperate climate also means year-round golf and tennis. If you're interested in diving or water skiing, or any other sport for which you need to hire equipment, ask at the tourist information offices in each town about the best places to do so.

ACTIVE SPORTS

Diving. Just off Sesimbra, south of Lisbon, the clear, calm waters are very good for snorkelling and scuba diving.

Fishing. All along the coast you will see anglers in boots casting off from the beaches, and others perched on rocks or man-made promontories. The best deep-sea fishing is for swordfish around the coast of Sesimbra (contact Marlin Boat Tours; http://marlin tours.com).

Golf. The Lisbon and Tagus Valley area has 18 courses, including top-rated Estoril Golf Club (18 holes; tel: 214-680 176), one of the oldest in the country, at Estoril; Estoril Sol Academia (9 holes; tel: 219-240 331) near Sintra; Lisbon Sports Club (18 holes; tel: 214-310

Canoes lined up at Praia dos Pescadores, Cascais

077) at Belas near Queluz; and Quinta da Marinha (18 holes; tel: 214-860 100; www.quintadamarinha.com) near Cascais, designed by Robert Trent Jones. Details on all the golf courses surrounding Lisbon can be found on www.portugalgolf.pt.

Riding. You can hire a horse, with or without an instructor, at the Clube Equestre de Janas (Rua do Alecrim, s/n, Sintra; 962-246 019) or at the Quinta da Marinha in Cascais (www.quintadamarinha.com), which also has an equestrian centre.

Sailing and boating. Most beaches protected from the open ocean have rowing boats, canoes or pedalos for rent by the hour. Experienced sailors in search of a more seaworthy craft should ask at the local yacht marina. Rowing boats are also available at Parque das Nações near the Oceanário.

Swimming. Because of pollution along the Estoril Coast, you should not swim in the sea any closer to Lisbon than at Estoril itself, which has been granted an EU blue flag. At Guincho and beyond,

Day trip to the beach

the sea is perfectly clean, but beware of the strong undertow. South of Lisbon from Caparica onwards is delightful, but can also be windy, with very rough seas. **Tennis**. Major hotels tend to have their own tennis courts, but there are tennis clubs and public courts as well. Many golf clubs also have tennis courts.

SPECTATOR SPORTS

Motor racing. Races and events take place at Estoril's Autodrome (www.circuito-estoril.pt).

Football (Soccer). Football draws big crowds in Portugal, and Lisbon's two major teams are Benfica and Sporting Clube de Portugal. Benfica plays at one of the most famous stadia in the world, the **Estádio da Luz, which** was built for and hosted the final of Euro 2004, when Portugal lost in a shock defeat to Greece. Benfica (officially called Sport Lisboa e Benfica) is the giant of Portuguese football who wins (together with Porto) most domestic trophies. The impressive **José Alvalade Stadium** near Campo Grande is home to Sporting Clube de Portugal, better known as Sporting Lisbon. Seating over 50,000 spectators, the stadium was built for Euro 2004 adjacent to the original stadium. The team usually plays second fiddle to city rivals Benfica, but still boasts an impressive array of trophies: over 18 league wins, 16 Portuguese Cup wins and a European Cup Winners Cup in 1964. If you fancy seeing some top-quality Portuguese football, tickets are generally not too difficult to get hold of (for Sporting tickets, www.sporting.pt; for Benfica tickets, www.slbenfica.pt).

CHILDREN'S ACTIVITIES

With its trams, elevators, funiculars, ferries and tourist trains, Lisbon offers some great ways to entertain children just by touring around the city. Take the Transtejo ferry to Cacilhas, a traditional tram to the castle or the metro to **Parque das Nações**, which has a splendid aquarium (Oceanário de Lisboa, see page 60), playgrounds, fountains, paddleboats and aerial cable cars. The **Planetário Calouste Gulbenkian** (http://ccm.marinha.pt/pt/planetario) in Belém (see page 52) has special planetarium shows for school children.

Football flags flying at Benfica

Another great place for kids is the **Jardim Zoológico de Lisboa** (Zoo, Praça Marechal Humberto Delgado; tel: 217-232 900/910; www.zoo.pt; daily 10am–6pm, until 8pm Apr–Sept). As well as elephants, tigers, giraffes and gorillas, there are boats and a miniature train, plus shows at various times of day when animals from pelicans to dolphins are fed. There is also **Tapada Nacional de Mafra**, a wildlife park with deer, wolves and wild boar at Mafra (www.tapada demafra.pt; daily 9am–5.30pm), some 40km north of the city.

Campo Grande, between the zoo and the airport, is a popular park. Palm, cedar and willow trees shade pretty walks, and there's a small lake with rowing boats.

For a safe beach with clean water you'll have to travel to Estoril or Cascais (see page 91). Alternatively, head south of the river to Caparica when the wind is light, or Sesimbra and Tróia otherwise.

Giraffes at the zoo

CALENDAR OF EVENTS

As you plan your excursions, it is worth checking details of festivals and fairs in and around Lisbon with tourist information offices.

January 1st New Year's Day dip at Carcavelos Beach.

February–March Carnival (Mardi Gras). Processions and fireworks.

March Moda Lisboa, Lisbon fashion week.

March–April Easter services and processions. Peixe em Lisboa food festival (http://peixemlisboa.com). Dias da Música em Belém, music festival at Centro Cultural de Belém (http://ccb.pt). Estoril Open ATP/WTA tennis tournament (http://millenniumestorilopen.com).

May Pilgrimage to Fátima (12–13 May). IndieLisboa, Portugal's biggest independent film festival (http://indielisboa.com). Arte Lisboa contemporary art fair (www.ifema.es/arco/lisboa).

May–June Rock in Rio (http://rockinriolisboa.sapo.pt; every two years), long-running rock festival featuring international stars.

May–Sept Out Jazz festival in parks and gardens around Oeiras (http://outjazz.pt).

June Festival of music, dance and theatre (all month). *Festas dos santos populares* (festivals of the popular saints) starting with St Anthony (13 June), on the eve of his feast day there's a costumed parade down the Avenida da Liberdade followed by celebrations in Alfama; the nights of St John (23 June) and St Peter (28 June) are almost as festive, and the season finishes with a burst of fireworks.

June–December Estoril Festival of international music (http://festorilisbon.com).

August Jazz em Agosto – jazz concerts at the Museu Gulbenkian (https://gulbenkian.pt/jazzemagosto). Cascais Sea Festival (Festas do Mar), with daily concerts and fireworks.

Sept–Oct Sintra music festival (http://festivaldesintra.pt), including live performances in the town's historic palaces and gardens.

November DocLisboa documentary film festival (http://doclisboa.org). Alkantara Art Festival, performing arts festival (http://alkantara.pt). Dia de São Martinho (St Martin's Day), when the year's new wine is tasted.

FOOD AND DRINK

The Lisbon dining scene has become much more diverse in recent years. The Bairro Alto is still one of the best areas for eating out, and is dense with restaurants of all kinds, especially small traditional dives. But as Lisbon moves to embrace the river again, restaurants have been popping up along the old dock areas and along the riverfront near the Parque das Nações. Another popular eating area is the rejuvenated Mercado da Ribeira, now home to the Time Out Market, and the surrounding streets (see page 86).

Seafood is perhaps the best thing to try, as there is a surfeit of fresh fish and shellfish. Not that restaurants skimp on meat: you can find delicious pork or lamb dishes and steak. More adventurous palates can try cuisines imported from Portugal's former African and Asian colonies.

A dish of carne de porco à Alentejana

Portions in Portuguese restaurants tend to be generous, and in the more traditional restaurants it's perfectly OK to order a half portion (which is usually charged at approximately two-thirds the full price) or a portion between two.

Even the top restaurants in Lisbon are fairly affordable by the standards of European capitals. The 'tourist menu' (ementa turística) in many restaurants, particularly at lunchtime, can be an excellent value at 15–20 euros. It is an economically priced set meal – typically bread, butter, soup, main course and dessert, with wine, beer, mineral water or a soft drink included.

RESTAURANTS AND MENUS

Lisbon's restaurants range from tiny *tascas* with bargain menus scrawled on boards to designer restaurants eyeing the latest Michelin awards, through bustling *cervejarias*, serving nothing but the freshest of seafood. Prices normally include taxes and a service charge, but you are expected to leave an extra five to 10 percent tip for good service.

Whether you indulge in one of Lisbon's chic riverfront restaurants or absorb some local colour in a simple backstreet family-run place, you can try a variety of dishes and cuisines from traditional Portuguese to tasty treats from the former colonies.

The prices displayed outside some of Lisbon's cafés may apply only if you stand at the bar. In Portugal, as in some other European countries, if you sit down at a table, you will have to pay the higher prices quoted on the regular menu. Also, in restaurants where seafood portions are charged by weight, waiters may bring out repeated portions without your specifically ordering more. If you don't want them, just tell the waiter, otherwise the bill might be quite a shock.

Free appetisers?

Most restaurants serve a *couvert* – unrequested appetisers such as cheese, ham and meat and fish pastes that appear to be free. They are not. You will be charged a few euros for these, but some, such as shellfish, can be much more expensive. If you do not touch them, you should not be charged for them. You may have to point this out; few people opt to abstain.

Salt and pepper

Salt and pepper are seldom put on the table. However, you will be given them if you ask: *Sal e pimenta, faz favor*.

MEALTIMES

Breakfast *(pequeno almoço)* is usually eaten any time until about 10am. **Lunch** *(almoço)* is served from shortly after noon until 3pm, and **dinner** *(jantar)* runs from 7.30 to 9.30pm (or later in a *casa de fado)*. Snacks between meals are usually taken at a *pastelaria* (pastry and cake shop), *salão de chá* (tea shop), or what the Portuguese call, in English, a *snack bar* – an over-the-counter bar, selling sandwiches, savoury pastries and sweets.

Because lunch and dinner tend to be major events, you may prefer the kind of light breakfast the Portuguese eat: coffee, toast or rolls, butter and jam. Larger hotels usually provide all the extras – such as juice, cereal, eggs and bacon.

SOUPS AND SEAFOOD

Soups. Lunch and dinner often get off to a solid start, and soups are hale-and-hearty typical Portuguese fare. *Caldo verde* (green soup) is a thick broth of potato purée with finely shredded cabbage or kale. Sometimes sausage is added. *Sopa à Portuguesa* is similar to *caldo verde*, but with added broccoli, turnips, beans, carrots and anything else the cook happens to have to hand. *Sopa de cozido* is a rich meat broth with cabbage and perhaps macaroni added. (This course is often followed by *cozido*, a huge serving of all the things that were boiled to create the broth, including beef, chicken, pork, sausages, potatoes, cabbage and carrots.) *Canja de galinha* is simple chicken-and-rice soup.

Seafood. The best advertisement for seafood is usually the window of a restaurant: a generous refrigerated display case with crabs and prawns, oysters and mussels, sea bass and sole. Seafood restaurants generally sell shellfish by the weight, giving the price in euros per kilo. The Portuguese are very fond of boiled and grilled fish dishes, usually served with generous portions of cabbage and boiled potatoes and doused with a little oil and vinegar.

A number of seafood dishes are true local specialities. *Caldeirada* is a rich seafood stew. *Amêijoas na cataplana* is an invention from the Algarve, of steamed clams (or mussels) with sausages, tomato, white wine, ham, onion and herbs. *Açorda de marisco* is a spicy, garlic-scented thick bread soup full of seafood bits; raw eggs are later added to the mixture. *Lulas recheadas* are squid stuffed with rice, olives, tomato, onion and herbs, though large squid *(chocos)* are often simply grilled. *Lampreia à Minho* is lamprey (similar to eel), not always highly regarded, but quite a delicacy in Portugal, served with a bed of rice and red wine sauce (best from January to March).

Seafood is in abundance

Sardinhas (sardines) are excellent in Lisbon and are often served charcoal-grilled *(sardinhas assadas)*.

Bacalhau (cod) is the national dish of Portugal, even though it can be expensive nowadays, and comes dried and salted, and from distant seas. The Portuguese say that cod is served in 100, 365 or 1,000 different ways, depending on the teller's taste for hyperbole. One of the best ways to try it is in *Bacalhau à Gomes de Sá*, in which flaky chunks are baked with parsley, potatoes, onion and olives and garnished with crumbled hard-boiled egg. Fresh fish, whole or filleted, is usually served grilled, as are *atum* (tuna) and *espadarte* (swordfish steaks). For those who know some Spanish or Portuguese, *peixe espada* might sound like swordfish but is actually scabbard fish, a long, thin fish that comes from the area south of Lisbon.

MEAT AND GAME

Bife na frigideira is not what you might think. *Frigideira* means frying pan, and this dish is beefsteak cooked in a wine sauce. *Cabrito assado* is baked kid served with rice and potato, heavy-going but delicious. *Carne de porco à Alentejana* is an inspired dish of clams and pork cooked with paprika and garlic. *Espetada mista* means Portuguese shish kebab: chunks of beef, lamb and pork on a spit. *Feijoada* is the national dish of Brazil, the former Portuguese colony. In Portugal, it's not nearly as elaborate or ritualised, but it's still a hearty and tasty stew of pigs' feet and sausage, white beans and cabbage.

Frango (chicken) is popular and prepared many ways: stewed in wine sauce, fried, roasted or barbecued to a tasty crisp (frango no

---

Market price

If you see '*preço V*' (or simply '*PV*') beside the seafood or shellfish on a menu, it means that the price is variable depending on the day's market price. Ask the price before ordering.

churrasco). Some restaurants specialise in game – *codorniz* (quail), *perdiz* (partridge), *lebre* (hare) and even *javali* (wild boar).

DESSERT AND CHEESE

The Portuguese have a sweet tooth. Portuguese cakes, custards and pastries made with egg yolks and sugar are delicious, especially the *pastéis de nata* (custard tarts). *Pudim flan* is the Portuguese version of crème caramel; it has many variations, including *Pudim de Marfim*. *Arroz doce* is rice pudding with a dash of cinnamon. *Maçã assada* is a tasty sugary baked apple. *Pudim Molotov* sounds like a bomb, and indeed it's so rich that it's sure to explode any strict diet – the fluffy egg-white mousse is immersed in a sticky caramel sauce.

And then there's cheese. The richest and most expensive in Portugal is *Serra da Estrela*, a delicious cured ewe's-milk cheese that originates high up in the mountains. You might also see *Flamengo*, a mild cheese very similar to Edam. Some restaurants serve *queijo*

Vintage port

A bottle of vintage port should be consumed within 48 hours of opening. At home or in Portugal, don't pay a high price for a glass of a rare vintage port unless the bartender or waiter opens the bottle in front of you. For most establishments, that's too expensive a proposition.

fresco as an appetiser. This is a small, white, soft mini-cheese made of ewe's and goat's milk, but it's fairly bland, so you may want to season it with pepper and salt.

INTERNATIONAL AND EXOTIC CUISINE

Portugal's cuisine is infused with tastes from other cultures, an advantage of its colonial baggage, which means that you can experiment with different cuisines while you're in Lisbon. The former colony of Goa accounts for the local popularity of *caril* (curry) and other Indian-style dishes. A typical Goan delicacy, a lot less pungent than Indian food, is *xacuti* (pronounced and sometimes spelled *chacuti*). The dish is simply chunks of fried chicken in a sauce of pepper, coriander, saffron, cinnamon, cumin, anise, cloves and coconut milk served with steamed rice. *Piri-piri* is a hot-pepper condiment and preparation from Angola that will set most mouths ablaze. Order a *piri-piri* dish with extreme caution.

Four centuries of ties with the territory of Macau assures all lovers of Chinese food a night out with dishes such as *gambas doces* (sweet-and-sour prawns).

TABLE WINES

Portuguese wines are generally good, and several regions produce truly excellent wines. Ask the waiter for *tinto* (red) or *branco* (white). *Vinho verde* (green wine), produced in the northwest, is like a young white wine, but fizzy, light and delightful. A lesser-known type is a red wine from the same region, bearing the seemingly oxymoronic name *vinho verde tinto* (red green wine). Both of these wines should be served chilled. *Vinhos maduros* are mature, or aged, wines.

Vinho espumante is Portuguese sparkling wine, packaged in a Champagne-shaped bottle. Most are sweet, but you can also find some quite dry versions.

All of the best wine-producing regions have names whose use is controlled by law *(região demarcada)*. You may come across these classifications: Bucelas, a light and fresh white wine; Colares, a traditional red wine; and Setúbal, a mellow, sweet white, sometimes served as an aperitif. Dão and Douro in the north produce vigorous reds and flavourful whites. Wines from the Alentejo region are also highly regarded.

The two most celebrated Portuguese wines, port and Madeira, are mostly known as dessert wines, but may also be sipped as aperitifs. The before-dinner varieties are dry or extra-dry white port and the dry Madeiras, *Sercial* and *Verdelho*. These should be served slightly chilled. After dinner, sip one of the famous tawny ports, or a Madeira dessert wine, *Boal* or *Malvasia* (malmsey).

OTHER DRINKS

Portuguese beers are good and refreshing. Light or dark, they are served chilled, bottled or from the tap. One of the best and most common brands is Sagres. *Aguardente* is the local brandy.

Barrels at a winery

Coffee is the main choice of beverage during the day and at the end of lunch or dinner. Most people order a *bica*, a small cup of black espresso coffee – also called simply *um café* or *um café espresso*. Tea (*chá*, pronounced 'shah'), by the bag, is also drunk – after all, it was the Portuguese explorers who first introduced it to the rest of the Western world. Although the concept of afternoon tea is generally regarded as British, its origins are in fact Portuguese, dating from 1662, when Catherine of Bragança, sister of Dom Afonso VI, married the English King Charles II. Her fashionable court popularised tea drinking.

PORT AND MADEIRA

Thanks to the unique growing conditions of the Douro Valley in the north of Portugal, fortified port wine has tantalised palates around the world since the British began exporting it in the 17th century. It differs from other wines due to the microclimate and soil of the region, and to the fact that the fermentation process is stopped with brandy. Traditionally the grapes picked each year were crushed in treading rooms by barefoot people, and a few vineyards still continue the tradition to this day. After two or three days' fermentation the brandy is added. The following spring, the fortified wine is sent to mature at the lodges on the banks of the River Douro at Vila Nova de Gaia (opposite Porto), from where it is shipped.

First produced on the island of Madeira in the 15th century, Madeira wine became an important export trade due to a combination of its notable quality and Madeira's position on the shipping lanes to the Indies. With the rise of the British colonies in North America and the West Indies, it fast became a favourite on both sides of the Atlantic. Madeira wine only became a fortified wine when, like port, it was decided to add grape brandy to stabilise it on long sea voyages.

TO HELP YOU ORDER...

Could we have a table? **Queremos uma mesa?**
Do you have a set-price menu? **Tem uma ementa turística?**
I'd like a/an/some… **Queria…**

beer **uma cerveja**
the bill a **conta**
bread **pão**
butter **manteiga**
dessert **sobremesa**
fish **peixe**
fruit **fruta**
ice-cream **gelado**
meat **carne**
the menu **a carta**
milk **leite**
mineral water **água mineral**

napkin **guardanapo**
pepper **pimenta**
potatoes **batatas**
salad **salada**
salt **sal**
sandwich **sanduíche**
soup **sopa**
sugar **açúcar**
tea **chá**
vegetables **legumes**
wine **vinho**
wine list **carta de vinos**

MENU READER

alho garlic
amêijoas baby clams
arroz rice
assado roast, baked
bacalhau cod
besugo sea bream
dobrada tripe
dourada sea bass
feijões beans
frito fried
gambas prawns
lagosta spiny lobster
lenguado sole

lombo fillet
lulas squid
mariscos shellfish
mexilhões mussels
ostras oysters
ovo egg
pescada hake
pescadinha whiting
polvos baby octopus
queijo cheese
salmonete red mullet
truta trout
vitela veal

WHERE TO EAT

The prices indicated here are for dinner with starter, main course and dessert, with wine, per person. (Note that some fish or shellfish dishes will be more expensive.) Tax (IVA) is included. All restaurants listed here accept major credit cards. Note that some Lisbon restaurants close for a week or two over the summer.

€€€€	over 45 euros
€€€	30–45 euros
€€	20–30 euros
€	below 20 euros

LISBON

Alfama

A Baiuca €€€ *Rua de São Miguel 20, tel: 939-457 098.* Open daily 8pm–midnight. This small, family-run Alfama restaurant offers good Portuguese fare and amateur fado performances.

Casanova €€ *Avda Infante Dom Henrique, Loja 7 Armazém B, Cais da Pedra à Bica do Sapato, tel: 218-877 532,* http://pizzeriacasanova.pt. Open daily 12.30pm–1.30am. Very popular Italian serving pizza, pasta and crostini accompanied by sumptuous river views from its terrace (at least when the cruise ships aren't docked to block the view). You can't book, so turn up early.

Chapitô á Mesa €€€ *Costa do Castelo 7, tel: 218-875 077,* http://chapito.org. Open Mon–Fri noon–midnight, Sat & Sun 7.30pm–midnight. This restaurant serves up hearty Portuguese food, and offers stunning views over the city.

Bairro Alto

100 Maneiras €€€€ *Rua do Teixeira 39, tel: 910-918 181,* www.100maneiras. com. Open Tue–Sat 7pm–1am. An intimate, elegant restaurant that is foodie heaven, offering various tasting menus (from €130); each dish is a surprise.

Chef Ljubomir Stanisic also has a less formal and cheaper bistro at 9 Largo de Trinidade in Chiado.

Cervejaria da Trindade €€€ *Rua Nova da Trindade 20, tel: 213-423 506,* www.cervejariatrindade.pt. Open daily noon–midnight. Recently renovated, this famous old beer hall and restaurant in a former monastery with *azulejo*-covered walls, serves extremely popular Portuguese dishes and seafood specialities at good prices; light bar snacks also available.

Páteo €€€€ *Bairro do Avillez, Rua Nova da Trindade 18, tel: 2153-830 290,* www.bairrodoavillez.pt. Open Daily 12.30–3pm & 7pm–midnight. Top chef José Avillez has four lively restaurants in this artfully converted former monastery: Páteo is at the heart of the "patio", a beautiful balconied space beneath soaring roof lights. It specialises in fish and seafood, with sublime dishes such as garlic prawns, fish rice and tuna escabeche, as well as a few meat and vegetarian dishes

Principe do Calhariz €€ *Calçada do Combro 28–30, tel: 213-420 971.* Open Mon–Fri & Sun noon–3pm & 7pm–midnight. This lively restaurant just beyond the Bica funicular, is a good place to discover local dishes, particularly from northern Portugal where the owners come from. Try *coelho à caçador* (rabbit, hunter's style) or Mirandesa veal steak.

Sea me Peixaria Mdoerna €€€ *Rua do Loreto 21, tel: 213-461 564,* www.peixariamoderna.com. Open daily 12.30–3.30pm & 7pm–midnight. This elegant and popular restaurant with simple décor and wooden tables offers a modern take on traditional seafood dishes inspired by Asian flavours. There is also a sushi bar. It has another branch at Time Out Market (Mercado da Ribeira).

Central Lisbon

Belcanto €€€€ *Rua Serpa Pinto 10a, tel: 213-420 607,* www.belcanto.pt. Open Tue–Sat 12.30–3pm & 7pm–midnight. This stylish restaurant with two Michelin stars is run by José Avillez, a renowned Portuguese chef, who offers a modern interpretation of traditional Portuguese cuisine using the best quality organic ingredients. The tasting menus are outstanding.

Casa do Alentejo €€ *Rua das Portas de Santo Antão 58, tel: 213-405 140*, www.casadoalentejo.pt. Open daily noon–3pm & 7–11pm. A centre dedicated to Alentejan culture, with its own restaurant, in a beautifully tiled upstairs dining room. Alentejo specialities include cod with chickpeas and carne de porco à alentejana (grilled pork with clams). Or you can just pop in for a drink in the superb bar or courtyard taverna.

Cafe Buenos Aires €€€ *Calçada Escadinhas do Duque 31 B, tel: 213-420 739*, www.cafebuenosaires.pt. Open Mon–Sat 6pm–1am. This shabby-chic Argentinian restaurant is a romantic, candlelit, atmospheric place to tuck into superlative steaks and delicious salads. It's perched beside a staircase leading steeply up from the Rossio towards Bairro Alto. Cash only.

Estórias na Casa da Comida €€€€ *Travessa das Amoreiras 1, tel: 213-860 889*, www.casadacomida.pt. Open Tue–Sat 7.30–10.30pm. An elegant restaurant in an old mansion, decorated in soft colours, in northwest Lisbon near the aqueduct. Fine Portuguese cuisine with a modern twist is served outdoors in a patio setting.

Gambrinus €€€€ *Rua das Portas de Santo Antão 23, tel: 213-421 466*, www.gambrinuslisboa.com. Open daily noon–midnight. A sophisticated restaurant, one of the city's finest and most famous, in a street of restaurants, close to Rossio. Specialises in traditional Portuguese and Galician dishes.

Martinho da Arcada €€€ *Arcadas do Terreiro do Paço/Praça do Comércio 3, tel: 218-879 259*, www.martinhodaarcada.pt. Open Mon–Sat noon–3pm & 7–10pm. Lisbon's oldest café, under the arcades at Praça do Comércio, dates back to 1782 and has a history littered with political and literary figures – it was a favourite of poet Fernando Pessoa.

Pap 'Açorda €€€€ *Avda 24 de Julho 49, tel: 213-464 811*, https://papacorda.com. Open Tue–Sun noon–midnight. Upstairs above the market hall, this is a cool but disarmingly informal restaurant, popular with a wide-ranging clientele. Traditional and creative Portuguese dishes, with fabulous and filling açorda real (a thick shellfish stew with lobster and shrimp) as the main speciality.

Ribadouro €€€ *Avda da Liberdade 155, tel: 213-549 411*, www.cervejariariba douro.pt. Open daily noon–1.30pm. The Avenida's best *cervejaria*, serving excellent seafood, including the superb speciality prawns with garlic and pricier lobster, crab, oysters and clams – they also do a decent *bacalhão* (salted cod) and an excellent gambas à bras (prawns with finely chipped potatoes). If you don't fancy a full meal, take a seat at the bar and order a beer with a plate of prawns. It's best to book for the restaurant, especially at weekends.

Tágide €€€€ *Largo da Academia Nacional de Belas Artes 19, tel: 213-404 010*, www.restaurantetagide.com. Open Tue–Sat 12.30–3pm & 7–11pm. Classic Portuguese and French restaurant west of the Praça do Comércio in an elegant, old house offering magnificent views of the waterfront, cathedral and square. There are Port wine tasting sessions and the tapas bar below offers cheaper lunch menu options.

A Travessa €€€ *Travessa do Convento das Bernardas 12, tel: 213-902 034*, http://atravessa.com. Open Mon–Sat 7.30–11.30pm. A Belgian- and French-influenced menu with dishes such as mussels, stuffed aubergine and bacon-wrapped dates enlivens this good-looking place near Parliament. Mussel feasts on Saturday nights.

York House Restaurant €€€€ *Rua das Janelas Verdes 32, tel: 213-962 435*, www.yorkhouselisboa.com. Open daily for breakfast (7.30–10.30am) and dinner (7.30–9.30pm); open for lunch Wed–Sun 12.30–3pm. Inhabiting a former 17th-century convent, now the refined and retreat-like York House Hotel, this is a cut above a typical hotel restaurant, with a refined atmosphere and a daily-changing menu featuring imaginative interpretations of Portuguese cuisine. There's also a beautiful leafy courtyard. Excellent desserts.

Bélem

Antigua Confeitaria de Belém € *Rua de Belém 84–92, tel: 213-637 423*, www. pasteisdebelem.pt. Open daily 8am–midnight. This legendary purveyor of custard tarts cooks up Lisbon's finest *pastéis de nata*, and its warren-like, tiled interior seats huge numbers of people, all wondering at the deliciousness of these still-warm, delicate pieces of heaven, made to a secret recipe.

MAAT Café and kitchen €€€ *Avenida de Brasilia, tel: 910 583 709*. Wed–Fri & Sun 11am–midnight, Sat 10am–1am. Sleek and stylish, the MAAT café and restaurant sit below the museum's sweeping roof, superbly framing the river views. The café, with outdoor seating, serves an array of drinks and snacks (the pastéis de nata are superb), while the adjacent restaurant specialises in expensive fish and seafood.

Portugalia €€€ *Avda de Brasilia Edif, Espelho d'Água, tel: 213-032 700,* www.portugalia.pt. Open daily noon–midnight. Marooned on a little island in an artificial lake facing the Padrão dos Descobrimentos, this glass-fronted restaurant, which is part of a popular chain, has a serene position. Dishes include *bitoques* (small steaks) from €11 and a wonderful gambas à brás (prawns with stick potatoes and onions).

São Jerónimo €€ *Rua dos Jerónimos 12, tel: 213-648 796*. Open Mon–Fri for lunch and dinner, Sat for dinner only. A sleek, beautifully designed restaurant with warm woods, dimmed lighting and leather chairs, just around the corner from the Jerónimos Monastery. The menu features creative Portuguese cuisine.

Solar dos Nubes €€€ *Rua dos Luciadas 70, tel: 213-647 359,* www.solardosnunes.com. Open Mon–Sat for lunch and dinner. This stylish restaurant has been awarded a Michelin Bib Gourmand. Offers traditional Portuguese fare and great wine list.

The Docks

Price ranges are the average for restaurants in the Docks.

A Praça €€€ *LX Factory, Edifício H, Espaço 001, tel: 210 991 792*. Open Daily 12.30–10.30pm. One of the larger restaurants in LX Factory, a hip spot with an open kitchen serving a range of dishes, including pasta, steaks and seafood. It also does good cocktails.

Capricciosa €€ *Doca de Santo Amaro Armazém 8, tel: 213-955 977,* www.capricciosa.com.pt. Open Mon–Thurs & Sun noon–midnight, Fri–Sat noon–1am. Set inside a bright former warehouse, Capricciosa serves good value artesan pizzas as well as pasta and salads. Next to a pedestrianized walkway around the marina, it's always popular with families; try and bag one of the tables facing the bobbing boats of the marina.

Último Porto €€ *Estação Marítima da Rocha Conde de Óbidos, tel: 213 979 498*. Open Mon–Sat noon–4pm. Perched at the edge of Lisbon's main container shipping docks, this earthy lunchtime restaurant ('the last port') is popular with the local dock workers who come here at lunchtimes for inexpensive and delicious grilled fish; the fresh sardines are hard to beat and portions are generous.

OUTSIDE LISBON

Cozinha Velha €€€€ *Palácio Nacional de Queluz, Largo do Palácio, Queluz, tel: 927-422 150, www.pousadas.pt*. Open Wed–Sun 12.30–3pm & 7.30–10pm. One of the most atmospheric restaurants in Portugal, this was once the old kitchen of the royal palace, but has now been converted into a dining room. It has a garden patio and a decor that will transport you to the 17th century. The regional cooking is excellent. Specialities include stewed partridge with chestnuts and grapes and goat's cheese with walnut and honey wrapped in pastry.

Lawrence Hotel €€€ *Rua Consigliéri Pedrosa 38–40, Sintra, tel: 219-105 500, http://lawrenceshotel.com*. Open daily 12–3.30pm & 7–9.30pm. The Dutch owners call this 'a restaurant with rooms' rather than a hotel, and Portugal's prime minister is among many who declare it their favourite place to eat. Opened in 1764, it's the oldest hotel in Portugal (Byron stayed here in 1809), and its restaurant is renowned.

Ponto Final €€€ *Rua do Ginjal 72, Almada, tel: 212 760 743*. Just across the Tagus River from Lisbon (via a 20-minute ferry ride from the Cais do Sodré ferry terminal and a short walk past abandoned warehouses) you'll find this oasis of a little restaurant. The dish to try here is the monkfish stew with rice that comes to your table bubbling in a clay pot. There's also a fantastic vegetarian version which includes tomato rice in a clay pot served with a side of crispy tempura green beans. Sitting just inches away from the water's edge with a crisp glass of *vinho verde*, you'll be glad you made the journey. Book ahead as it gets busy.

TRAVEL ESSENTIALS

PRACTICAL INFORMATION

A

ACCESSIBLE TRAVEL

Lisbon's cobbled streets and steep hills don't make it easy for wheelchair users, but areas such as Belém, Baixa and especially Parque das Nações are easier to get around, as they're flat with broad streets and pavements. Some Metro stations, but not all, are equipped for the visually and hearing impaired. To discover which have facilities for the disabled, visit www.metrolisboa.pt. Carris also offer a bus service, for those with reduced mobility, for which you will need to book ahead. Accessible Portugal (www.accessibleportugal.com) offer holidays for people with disabilities.

ACCOMMODATION (see also Camping, Youth hostels and Recommended hotels on page)

Hotels in Portugal are graded from 2-star to 5-star deluxe. The rates are lower in less elaborate places, such as an *estalagem* or inn; a *pensão* (rooms with meals available); a *residencial* (rooms, generally without meals); or an *alojamento local* (guesthouse).

Pousadas are a chain of hotels in converted historic buildings and scenic sites, now run by the Pestana chain. Ask at tourist offices (see page 131) for a detailed list, or visit the website www.pousadas.pt. Lisbon also now has a good selection of boutique-style hotels with modern facilities in historic buildings.

High season runs from mid-June to September, when you should book well ahead, but if a low-season visit is an option, prices are much lower then, and discounts are usually available for longer stays.

When you arrive at your accommodation, you'll usually be asked for your passport and to sign a form which sets out the conditions, prices and room number.

A double/single room **um quarto duplo/simples**

AIRPORT (see also Getting there)

The Aeroporto de Lisboa (www.ana.pt) is only 7km (4 miles) from the city centre, a 15-minute drive (allow twice as long at rush hour). There is a helpful tourist information office at the airport.

The Metro runs from the airport, which is the terminus of the red line from Sãn Sebastião. It takes around 21 minutes to the city centre. The AeroBus airport shuttle Line #1, leaves about every 20 minutes, 7.40am–10.30pm (from Cais do Sodré) and 8am–9pm (from the airport). It passes through the city centre, stopping at Rossio on the way to Cais do Sodré train station. The ticket (€4) can be used all day on trams and buses (though not the Metro). Local bus #744 to Pombal also calls at the airport (€1.50). The AeroShuttle Line #2 runs to the coach terminal at Sete Rios (€4), every half hour, 8am–7pm. Taxis are plentiful, and charge about €15–20 to the centre of Lisbon.

> Where do I get the bus to the airport/to the centre of Lisbon?
> **Onde posso apanhar o autocarro para o aeroporto/para o centro da cidade?**

B

BUDGETING FOR YOUR TRIP

Accommodation. At top levels, hotels in Lisbon compare to those in other large European cities. Still, there are some good prices to be found. A 2-star hotel should be €80–100 for a double; a 3-star €100–150; and for a 4-star, expect to pay over €200.

In three categories – historic, design and monuments – *pousadas* are usually priced like 4-star hotels, though the most in-demand historic ones may go higher. Prices usually drop in winter (1 November–1 April). Most prices include breakfast and 6 percent IVA tax (VAT).

Entertainment. Nightclubs covers are high (€10–20), as are drinks once inside (€7.50 and up). Concert tickets generally range from €10–45.

Flights. Around £100–200 from London.

Local transport. Public transport within the city – buses, trams and the Metro – is not that expensive, with single Metro fares at €1.50, and taxis are affordable and a good way to get around. Most taxi rides within Lisbon's major neighbourhoods will cost no more than €10. Trains to the Estoril Coast are inexpensive (Sintra, €5.80 return).

Meals. Even top-rated restaurants may be affordable compared to most European capitals. Portugal offers a midday meal bargain, the *menu* or *ementa turística*, often no more than €15 for a fixed-price, three-course meal. Portuguese wines are good and attractively priced (€10–20), even in fine restaurants. The house wine *(vinho da casa)* is normally good. A three-course dinner in a moderately priced restaurant (for one, with wine) should cost between €25–€35. For an expensive meal in one of Lisbon's prestigious restaurants, expect to pay €50 and up per person.

Museums. Admission fees range about €5–10; some days are free. Other sites and attractions may cost between €3 and €10. A Lisboa Card (see page 12) gives discounts.

Sports. Golfing can be expensive, though the courses are excellent: green fees go up to €100. Horse riding costs up to €50 a session.

C

CAMPING

There are several campsites in the Lisbon area, with facilities ranging from basic to elaborate. **Camping Lisboa** (Parque Municipal de Campismo de Monsanto) has 400 individual camping bays and additional bungalows, mobile homes for hire, on-site restaurant and a minimarket. There's also plenty of activities on offer with a swimming pool, tennis courts, mini golf and a gym. It's in Monsanto Park, at Estrada de Circunvalação 1500; tel: 217-628 200; www.lisboacamping.com.

Information can be obtained from tourist offices (see page 131) or the Federação Portuguesa de Campismo, Avenida Coronel Eduardo Galhardo 24D; tel: 218-126 890; www.fcmportugal.com.

CAR HIRE (see also Driving)

Major international firms Avis/Budget, Hertz, Sixt and Europcar have desks at the airport and locations in Lisbon; sometimes they also have small satellite offices in other towns. Hotels may recommend local, inexpensive operators. Many companies offer discounts if you book online in advance.

The minimum age for hiring a car is 21–25 (depends on the company), and anyone hiring one must have held a valid licence for at least one year. Rental companies will accept your home country's national driving licence, and you must show your passport. Third-party insurance should be included in the basic charge, but a collision-damage waiver and personal accident policy may be added.

A sub-compact, four-door car with manual transmission, air conditioning, unlimited mileage and mandatory liability insurance usually costs between €200 and €300 per week. Costs may rise in high season (Easter and summer months). Pick-up and drop-off at different points is acceptable without surcharge, though doing either at the airport will incur a supplement.

Avis/Budget: tel: 21 843 550; www.avis.com.pt / www.budget.com.pt
Europcar: tel: 21 840-11 76; www.europcar.com.
Hertz: tel: 21 942-63 00; www.hertz.pt.
Sixt: tel: 218-407 927; www.sixt.com.

I'd like to hire a car **Queria alugar um carro**
today/tomorrow **para hoje/amanhã**
for one day/a week **por um dia/uma semana**

CHILDREN

Portugal is a seriously child friendly country. Children are made welcome just about everywhere, including hotels, restaurants and bars. Watch the strength of the sun in summer months; always ensure your child is wearing a hat and plenty of sunblock. Children's meals are not always available but most restaurants are happy to provide a smaller portion. On public transport children under five travel free, while 4–12-year-olds pay half fare (on trains only).

CLIMATE

Lisbon has an Atlantic climate influenced by the Mediterranean, which produces hot summers and mild winters. Spring and autumn are the best seasons to be in Lisbon, but in the summer, you can bask in the sunshine at the beaches west and south of the capital. The table below gives average air temperatures per month.

	J	F	M	A	M	J	J	A	S	O	N	D
°C	12	12	14	15	18	21	23	24	22	18	15	13
°F	54	54	57	59	64	69	73	75	72	64	59	55

CLOTHING

Unless you come to Lisbon in an unseasonably cold winter, you'll never really have to dress warmly. Spring and autumn are relatively warm, so you won't need anything heavier than a sweater in the daytime and light jacket at night. Summer days can be quite hot, but pack a wrap or sweater for cooler, windy evenings, and rainwear, just in case. An umbrella may be useful in the winter months.

Lisboetas take care over their attire and tend to dress fashionably and fairly formally, but virtually no establishments require a tie. The Estoril Casino 'recommends' that men wear jackets in the evenings. It is respectful not to flash flesh (cover arms and legs) when visiting churches.

CRIME AND SAFETY (see also Emergencies and Police)

Lisbon traditionally has been one of Europe's more laid-back and safe cities, but you should still take the usual precautions. Carry valuables in inside pockets and keep your handbag or camera bag firmly under your arm. Stay alert for pickpockets on buses, trams and in cafés on Rossio, the Alfama area, markets and other tourist spots.

In most parts of the Baixa and Bairro Alto, it is safe to walk at night. Take care around the occasionally seedy Rossio square and narrow, dark and easy-to-get-lost-in streets of the Alfama district at night; if you are going to a *fado* house in the latter, you can take a taxi and have one called when you leave.

The beaches of the Estoril Coast outside Lisbon are quite safe, but it is not a good idea to take any valuables, cameras or purses to the beach. As a general rule, keep valuables in the hotel safe, and refrain from carrying large sums of money or wearing expensive jewellery. Report any theft to the hotel receptionist, the nearest police station or the local tourist office. Leave nothing of value in parked cars, the easiest target for thieves; always lock cars and never leave cases, bags, cameras, etc. in view.

CUSTOMS REGULATIONS

You can bring currency up to €10,000 into the country without declaration. The duty-free allowance for travellers over 17 years of age from non EU countries is 200 cigarettes and 1 litre of spirits or 4 litres of wine. EU residents can bring in 800 cigarettes, plus 10 litres of spirits, 20 litres of fortified wine, 20 litres of sparkling wine, 90 litres of still wine or 110 litres of beer.

D

DRIVING (see also Car hire)

It is not as tricky driving in Lisbon as some other European capitals, though traffic can be heavy and parking difficult. However, for most visitors, public transport and private taxis are vastly superior methods of navigating the city. To bring your own car into Portugal, you will need your national driving licence, registration papers and insurance – third-party cover is obligatory – and the Green Card that makes your insurance valid in other countries.

Road conditions. The main roads of Portugal are generally in good repair. In order of importance, they are graded as follows: *Auto-Estrada*: motorways (A1–A2, etc.); *Itinerário Principal*: highways (IP); *Itinerário Complementar*: Principal Route (IC); and *Estrada Nacional*: national roads (EN).

Rules and regulations. The rules of the road are the same as in most western European countries. Drive on the right. At roundabouts the vehicle already on the roundabout has priority unless road markings or lights indicate otherwise. Seat belts are compulsory and a heavy fine can be imposed if you are not wearing one.

Speed limits are 120km/h (75mph) on motorways, 100km on roads restricted to motor vehicles, 90km/h (56mph) on other roads and 50km/h (37mph) in urban areas. Minimum speeds are posted (in blue) for some motorway lanes and the suspension bridge across the Tagus. Most motorways have tolls.

Parking. Unless there's an indication to the contrary, you can park for as long as you wish. Certain areas are metered. In 'Blue Zones', you must buy a ticket from a machine for a designated time period; the ticket should then be displayed on the dashboard of the parked car. Car parks and garages are also available. There is a large car park at Gare do Oriente, if you don't want to bring your vehicle into the centre of the city.

Road signs. Standard international pictograms are used but you may encounter the following signs:

cruzamento crossroads
curva perigosa dangerous bend (curve)
descida ingreme steep hill
desvio diversion (detour)
estacionamento permitido parking allowed
estacionamento proíbido no parking
guiar com cuidado drive with care
paragem bus stop
pare stop
passagem proíbida no entry
pedestres/peões pedestrians
perigo danger
proibida a entrada no entry
seguir pela direita/esquerda keep right/left
sem saída no through road
sentido proíbido no entry
sentido único one-way street
trabalhos roadworks (men at work)
velocidade máxima maximum speed

If you need help. If you belong to a motoring organisation that is affiliated to the Automóvel Clube de Portugal (tel: 215-915 915, 707-509 510, www.acp. pt), you can use their emergency and repair services free of charge. Check online for details.

> Are we on the right road for…? **É esta a estrada para…?**
> Check the oil/tyres/battery, please **Verifique o óleo/os pneus/a bateria, se faz favor.**
> I've broken down. **O meu carro está avariado.**
> There's been an accident. **Houve um acidente.**

E

ELECTRICITY

Standard throughout Portugal is 220v, 50-cycle AC. For US appliances, 220v transformers and plug adaptors are needed.

EMBASSIES AND CONSULATES

Most embassies and consulates are open Mon–Fri from 9 or 10am until 5pm, with a break in the middle of the day of 1–2 hours.

Australia: Avenida da Liberdade 200, 2°, tel: 213-101 500.
Canada: Avenida da Liberdade 198-200, 3°, tel: 213-164 600.
Ireland: Avenida da Liberdade 200, 4°, tel: 213-308 200.
South Africa: Avenida Luís Bivar 10, tel: 213-192 200.
UK: Rua de São Bernardo 33, tel: 213-924 000.
US: Avenida das Forças Armadas 16, tel: 217-273 300.

EMERGENCIES *(see also Police)*

The following number is the general emergency number for use 24 hours a day in an emergency:

Police, fire and ambulance **112**

ETIQUETTE

The Portuguese are usually courteous and hospitable. Taking a short while to learn and use the language basics will serve you well. If you are invited to someone's house, it is polite to bring flowers for the hostess. There are always orderly queues at bus stops. Be certain to respect them. Stretching in public is considered rude. Otherwise, use common sense and a smile and you shouldn't go far wrong.

G

GETTING THERE (see also Airport)

By air. Lisbon's airport is linked by regularly scheduled daily non-stop flights from several European cities and from the East Coast of the United States. Flights from Canada, Australia and New Zealand go through London or another European capital.

TAP/Air Portugal (www.tap.pt) is Portugal's national airline. There are regular TAP and British Airways (www.ba.com) scheduled flights from the UK to Lisbon. Budget airlines offering services from the UK to Lisbon include easyJet (from London Gatwick, Luton and Bristol; www.easyjet.com) and Ryanair (from London Stansted, Birmingham, Edinburgh and Manchester; www.ryanair.com). From the US to Lisbon, TAP flies direct from New York, Miami, Chicago, San Francisco and Boston. United (www.united.com) flies direct from Newark. There are flights to the Portuguese capital on TAP and other carriers from all major European cities.

By sea. Lisbon is a major port, and several cruise ships include a port of call in the capital. Ferries from Great Britain go to Santander and Bilbao, Spain, from Plymouth and Portsmouth (Brittany Ferries; www.brittany-ferries.com). Crossings take 24–36 hours. The drive from northern Spain to Lisbon is then likely to take another 8 hours of non-stop driving.

By rail. Portugal is linked to the European railway network and connections to Lisbon are possible from points throughout Spain, France and the rest of continental Europe. Travel to Portugal is included on the InterRail Global Pass (www.interrail.eu) for Europeans, and the Eurail Global Pass (www.eurail.com) for non-Europeans.

The Portuguese national railway network is called **Caminhos de Ferro Portugueses** (www.cp.pt). Oriente station (Parque das Nações) serves all international trains.

Incredibly there is no direct train between Lisbon and its nearest European capital, Madrid. The 460- mile journey currently involves changing trains twice and takes at least ten hours. Both Spain and Portugal are building new high-speed tracks, and a fast direct train is expected by sometime in 2024. Still, one of the quickest, cheapest and most convenient ways to travel between cities is by plane.

By car. Major motorways connect Portugal with Spain at numerous border points. The fastest route from Oporto is the A1 *autoestrada*; to Madrid, take the A2 and A6 via Badajoz. The drive from Madrid to Lisbon takes around 6 hours; from Paris, it's 17–20 hours.

GUIDES AND TOURS

Information on tours currently on offer is available at tourist offices or from your hotel.

Yellow Buses (www.yellowbustours.com) offer tours around various parts of the city, including the Hills Tram tour on a historic tram (€20), a bus and tram tour which includes a bus to Belém and Parque das Naçoes (€35), and a boat, bus and tram tour taking in the above and a ride on the river (€45). Each tour lasts around 90 minutes, tickets are valid for at least 24 hours and include free use of Lisbon's other trams and funiculars.

Cityrama-Grayline (www.cityrama.pt) open-top bus tours start from Praça Marquês de Pombal.

All of the major excursion firms offer trips to Cascais, Estoril, Mafra, Queluz and Sintra, as well as a long day's outing covering major sites north of Lisbon: Fátima, Alcobaça and Batalha, Óbidos and Nazaré. If you are travelling independently, you can cover all these at greater leisure, even making an overnight stop or two on the way.

Transtejo runs regular ferries across the River Tagus, including from Cais do Sodré to Cacilhas and between Belém and Porto Brandhão (www.transtejo.pt).

H

HEALTH AND MEDICAL CARE

Standards of hygiene in Lisbon, and in Portugal as a whole, are generally very high; the most likely illness to befall travellers will be due to an excess of sun or alcohol. The water is safe to drink, but bottled water is available everywhere. Ask for *água com gas* (carbonated) or *sem gas* (still).

Farmácias (chemists/drugstores) are open during normal business hours, and one shop in each neighbourhood is on duty round the clock. Addresses are listed in newspapers and on pharmacy doors. To locate night pharmacies, tel: 118.

For more serious illness or injuries, the most central hospital is Hospital de Santa Maria (Avenida Prof. Egas Moniz 217 805 000, www.chin.min-saude. pt), and there are various other public hospitals around the city. Check your medical insurance to be sure it covers illness or accident while you are abroad. EU nationals with a European Health Insurance Card (EHIC) can receive free emergency treatment at Social Security and Municipal hospitals in Portugal. UK nationals need the Global Health Insurance Card (GHIC; www.nhs.uk). Privately billed hospital visits are expensive.

I need a doctor/dentist **Preciso de um médico/ dentista**
Get a doctor quickly. **Chame um médico, depressa.**
Where's the nearest pharmacy? **Aonde é a farmácia (de guardia) mais perto?**
an ambulance **uma ambulância**
hospital **hospital**
upset stomach **mal de estômago**
sunstroke **uma insolação**
fever **febre**

L

LANGUAGE

Portuguese, a derivative of Latin, is spoken in Brazil, Angola, Mozambique and Macau – all former colonies of Portugal. Any high-school Spanish may help with signs and menus, but will not unlock the mysteries of spoken Portuguese. The Portuguese spoken in Portugal is much more closed and gutteral-sounding, and is also spoken much faster than in Brazil.

Almost everyone in Portugal understands Spanish, some speak French and many people in Lisbon can speak good English. Schoolchildren are mostly taught English.

The *Berlitz Portuguese Phrasebook* covers most situations you're likely to encounter during a visit to Portugal. Also useful is the *Berlitz Portuguese–English/English–Portuguese Pocket Dictionary*, containing a menu-reader supplement (www.berlitzpublishing.com).

LGBTQ+ TRAVELLERS

Lisbon is the most important city in Portugal's gay scene, and offers a number of bars and clubs catering for a gay crowd, including the long-established Trumps club (Rua da Impressa Nacional 104; www.trumps.pt); the scene centres around Praça do Príncipe Real, close to Bairro Alto. Also, on the Costa da Caparica, the west coast of the peninsula across the Tagus, beach No. 9 on the narrow-gauge railway is also a popular hangout.

The Centro Comunitário Gay e Lésbico de Lisboa at Rua dos Fanqueieros 40 (tel: 218 873 918; Wed– Sat 7–11pm) is the main gay and lesbian community centre, run by ILGA, whose website (www.ilga-portugal.pt) is in Portuguese. A useful website with information on travel, bars and beaches is www.portugalgay.pt.

LOST PROPERTY

Report any loss to the **tourist police** station in the Foz Cultura building in Palácio Foz, Praça dos Restauradores (daily 24hr tel: 213 421 634). For items left on public transport, contact www.carris.pt.

Do you speak English? **Fala inglês?**
excuse me/you're welcome **perdão/de nada**
please **faz favor**
thank you **obrigado/a**
where/when/how **onde/quando/como**
day/week/month/year **dia/semana/mês/ano**
no/yes não/sim
left/right **esquerda/direita**
up/down acima/baixa
near/far **perto/longe**
cheap/expensive **barato/caro**
open/closed **aberto/fechado**
hot/cold **quente/frio**
old/new **velho/novo**
Please write it down. **Escreva-lo, por favor.**
What does this mean? **Que quer dizer isto?**
Help me, please. **Ajude-me, por favor.**
Just a minute. **Um momento.**
What time is it? **Que horas são?**
Days:
Sunday **domingo**
Monday **segunda-feira**
Tuesday **terça-feira**
Wednesday **quarta-feira**
Thursday **quinta-feira**
Friday **sexta-feira**
Saturday **sábado**
What day is it today? **Que dia é hoje?**
yesterday **ontem**
today **hoje**
tomorrow **amanhã**

M

MAPS

Tourist information offices have free maps of Lisbon and the surrounding area, as well as a Carris map of the tram, bus and elevator network. Towns on the tourist circuit, such as Óbidos, Sintra, Cascais and Estoril, also make free maps available through their tourist information offices.

MEDIA

Europe's principal newspapers, including most British dailies, and the *International Herald Tribune*, are available on the day of publication at many newsagents and hotels. Popular foreign magazines are also sold at the same shops or stands. The most important Portuguese-language daily are Correio da Manhã and *Diário de Notícias*, which contains cultural listings.

Free listings publications, such as *Follow Me Lisboa and Agenda Cultural Lisboa*, are widely available. *Portugal News*, an English-language weekly published in the Algarve, covers stories from around the country (www.the portugalnews.com).

Foreign films, whether made-for-TV or original cinematic productions, are usually shown in the original language with subtitles. Most hotels have access to satellite TV.

MONEY

Currency *(moeda)*. The euro (€) is the official currency used in Portugal. Notes are denominated in 5, 10, 20, 50, 100, 200 and 500 euros; coins in 1 and 2 euros and 1, 2, 5, 10, 20 and 50 cents *(centimos)*.

Currency exchange *(banco, câmbio)*. Normal banking hours are Mon–Fri 8.30am–3pm. There is a 24-hour exchange office at the airport.

Credit cards *(cartão de crédito)*. International credit cards are widely accepted. However, in some shops and restaurants, especially in small towns outside Lisbon, you may not be able to use a credit card.

Tax refunds. For non-EU residents, the IVA tax (VAT) imposed on most goods can be refunded on purchases of at least €61.50 in a single store. Look for the blue-and-white tax-free sign in stores. To obtain the rebate, fill in a form provided by the shop where you purchase the goods. One copy is kept by the shop; the others must be presented at customs upon departure. The refund can be credited to your credit card at the airport or posted to your home address after your return.

Can I pay with this credit card? **Posso pagar com cartão de crédito?**
I want to change some pounds/dollars. **Queria trocar libras/ dólares.**
Can you cash a travellers' cheque? **Pode pagar um cheque de viagem?**

OPENING HOURS

Banks open Monday to Friday 8.30am–3pm, and closed at weekends and on bank holidays. Most **shops** open Monday to Saturday 9am–7pm; smaller shops close for lunch (around 1–3pm) and on Saturday afternoons. Many **shopping centres** around Lisbon and the suburbs open on Sundays and have extended opening hours, closing at 10pm or midnight during the week. Most **museums** and **monuments** open Tuesday to Sunday from around 10am–6pm; details are given in the Guide, or check individual websites.

POLICE (see also Crime and safety and Emergencies)

The Portuguese national police, identified by their blue uniforms, are generally helpful and friendly, and often speak a little English. Policemen assigned to traffic duty wear red armbands with a silver letter 'T' (for *trânsito*, or traffic) on a red background.

On highways, traffic is controlled by the Guarda Nacional Republicana (GNR) in white-and-red or white-and-blue cars, or on motorcycles. Occasionally they make spot-checks on documents or tyres, and can issue on-the-spot fines.

Lisbon's tourist police are based in the Palacio Foz, Praca dos Restauradores (tel: 213-421 623 or 213-400 090), and can help with any crimes or wrongdoing against tourists. They should be your first port of call in case of theft or any minor misdemeanour. The emergency number is **112**.

Where's the nearest police station? **Onde fica o posto de polícia mais próximo?**

POST OFFICES

The mail service is efficient, with British-style red pillar boxes. **Post offices** (*correios*) are usually open Monday to Friday 8.30am–6.30pm. Some major branch offices also operate on Sat until noon. A 24-hour office can be found at the airport. Lisbon's main post office is in Praça dos Restauradores 58(opposite the tourist office). You can purchase stamps from post offices as well as at some tobacconists and kiosks, and anywhere that displays the sign "Correio de Portugal – Selos".

A stamp for this letter/postcard, please. **Um selo para esta carta/ este postal, por favor.**

PUBLIC HOLIDAYS

1 January *Ano Novo* New Year's Day
25 April *Dia da Liberdade* 1974 Revolution Day
1 May *Dia do Trabalhador* May Day

10 June *Dia de Camões* Camões's Day

15 August *Assunção* The Assumption

5 October *Implantaçao da República* Republic Day

1 November *Todos-os-Santos* All Saints' Day

1 December *Dia da Indepêndencia* Independence Day

8 December *Imaculada Conceição* Immaculate Conception

25 December *Natal* Christmas Day

Moveable dates

Carnaval (Shrove Tuesday/Carnival), *Sexta-feira Santa* (Good Friday), *Domingo de Páscoa* (Easter Sunday) and *Corpo de Deus* (Corpus Christi).

Local holidays

Lisbon, Estoril and Cascais have a local holiday on 13 June in honour of St Anthony (Santo António). Sintra has a holiday on 29 June (São Pedro).

R

RELIGION

The Portuguese are predominantly Roman Catholic, a fact reflected in surviving religious rituals and saints' days that are public holidays. The shrine at Fátima is one of the most important pilgrimages in Catholicism. The tourist information office has a list of services for English-speaking Catholics as well as other services. Dress modestly when visiting religious sites.

T

TELEPHONES

Portugal's country code is **351**. The local area code – **21** in the case of Lisbon and the Estoril Coast, including Sintra – must be dialled before all phone numbers, including local calls (nine digits in total).

Most European **mobile phones** will work in Lisbon, and those with mobiles from EU countries will pay no additional roaming charges. If your phone is not from an EU country and you're spending a lot of time in Portugal, you may find it cheaper to buy a local SIM card from a phone shop or kiosk.

Note that local, national and international calls made from hotels almost always carry an exorbitant surcharge.

Dialling internationally is straightforward: dial 00 for an international line (both Europe and overseas) plus the country code (UK 44, US 1) plus the phone number (including the area code, without the initial '0' where there is one).

TIME ZONES

Portugal, being at the western edge of Europe, maintains Greenwich Mean Time (GMT), along with the UK, and is therefore one hour behind the rest of the EU. From the last Sunday in March until the last Sun in October, the clocks are moved one hour ahead for summer time, GMT + 1.

In summer the chart looks like this:

New York	London	**Lisbon**	Paris	Sydney	Auckland
7am	noon	**noon**	1pm	9pm	11pm

TIPPING

Hotel and restaurant bills are generally all-inclusive, but an additional tip of 5–10 percent is common.

Hotel porters generally receive around €0.50–€1 for each bag that they carry, while hairdressers and taxi drivers are normally tipped about 10 percent and tour guides 10–15 percent. Toilet attendants should be tipped about €1 and your hotel room cleaner should be given around an extra €1 per day.

TOILETS

Public toilets can be found in many public places, including stations, museums and large stores. Toilets are marked *Senhoras* (ladies) and *Homens* (men).

Where are the toilets? **Onde é o lavabo/quarto de banho?**

TOURIST INFORMATION

Before you travel, the websites www.turismodeportugal.pt and www.visit portugal.com are useful sources of information.

In Lisbon itself, the main tourist information office for the city is the **Lisboa Welcome Centre**, at Praça do Comércio Loja 1, tel: 210-312 810, www.visit lisboa.com. The main Portugal tourist office, which can also provide information about the city as well is in the **Palácio Foz**, on the west side of Praça dos Restauradores, tel: 213-463 314. Tourist offices at the **Airport Arrivals Terminal** (tel: 218-450 660) and at **Santa Apolónia station** (tel: 910-517 982) can help with finding accommodation, as can a few smaller "Ask Me" terminals dotted around the city.

Where is the tourist office? **Onde é o turismo?**

TRANSPORT

Buses: Local. You can get a free map of the entire transit system at tourist information offices, or online at the **Carris** website (www.carris.pt), the transport authority. You can either use a Viva Viagem pass (see below) – just scan your pass at the machine as you enter the bus – or you can buy a single ticket from the driver.

Buses: Inter-city. The main inter-city bus terminal "Terminal Rodoviário" is at Sete Rios, by the zoo, and serves towns and cities around the country. Ask for information about bus routes at the tourist office in Praça dos Restauradores.

Trams. Tram stops are indicated by large signs marked *paragem* (stop). The Carris bus map shows tram routes as well. The most popular tourist tram is the No. 28, which goes from Bairro Alto to Alfama and the castle. Most trams are entered at the front, where you buy a ticket from the driver, or you can use your pass.

Metro. Lisbon's underground Metropolitano (www.metrolisboa.pt) has four colour-coded lines. The red line runs all the way to the airport. Certain stations link up with railway stations and ferry terminal.

Tickets and fares. The cheapest way to travel on the trams, Metro and local buses is to buy an electronic Viva Viagem card (€0.50), available at station vending machines and ticket offices, which you then charge up as you go. You can load it up with between €3–40, after which €1.50 is deducted for each bus or metro journey. You can also charge it for a 24-hour session (*bilhete 1-dia*), which costs €6.40 (or €10.60 including trains to Sintra and Cascais) and is valid for unlimited journeys on the Metro and Carris networks (the latter includes funiculars such as the Elevador de Santa Justa). Children under four travel free on the Metro.

Trains. Lisbon has four railway stations. The main ones for national and international travel are Santa Apolónia (reached by bus No. 9 or 9A from Avenida da Liberdade) and Estação do Oriente (Oriente Metro). Commuter trains for the western suburbs, Estoril and Cascais depart from Cais do Sodré, on the waterfront, while trains for Sintra and the west depart from Rossio station.

How much is a ticket to…? **Quanto é o bilhete para …?**
Will you tell me when to get off? **Pode dizer-me quando devo descer?**
Where's the nearest bus/tram stop? **Onde fica a mais próxima paragem dos autocarros/eléctricos?**
Where can I get a taxi? **Onde posso encontrar um táxi?**
What's the fare to…? **Quanto custa o percurso até …?**

Taxis. Lisbon's metered taxis, often Mercedes, are cream, and indicated by a sign reading TAXI. The fare is shown on the meter – check that it's running. Drivers add 20 percent from 9pm to 6am and bags in the boot incur a €1.60 fee. Outside the rush hour taxis can be flagged down quite easily, or head for one of the ranks such as those outside the main train stations. At night, it's best to phone a taxi (attracts an extra charge of €0.80): try Teletaxis (tel: 218-111 100, www.teletaxis.pt). Uber also operates in Lisbon and fares are similar to the city cabs.

Ferries. The two main ferry stations for the River Tagus's southern shore are Estação Fluvial Terreiro do Paço for Barreiro, and Cais do Sodré for Cacilhas, Montijo and Seixal.

Bikes. Most of Lisbon is very hilly, but the riverfront is flat and good for cycling. Lisbon has a citywide bike-sharing scheme run by Gira (www.gira-biciclet-asdelisboa.pt), and there are bike hire outlets at Belém and Doca de Santo Amaro (Armazém 7, 218 250 266; daily 10am–7pm). Expect to pay around €5 an hour.

V

VISAS AND ENTRY REQUIREMENTS

You need a valid passport for a visit to Portugal. EU citizens don't need a visa and can stay in the country as long as they like. Some non-EU citizens, including those from the UK, US, Canada, Australia and New Zealand, can stay for up to 90 days without a visa. All other foreign nationals need to check individual entry requirements and may need to apply for a visa.

Currency restrictions. If you are travelling to or from a country outside the European Union you must declare if you are carrying over €10,000 in cash (or the equivalent in other currencies).

Customs. If you are a non-EU resident, you may be able to reclaim VAT on some items bought within Portugal – look out for shops with the sign 'Tax Free Shopping' in the window. The minimum spend in one store on the same day is €61.50. You will need to complete a form and present it when you are leaving the country, along with the purchased goods. There are no duty-free allowances for EU citizens travelling within the EU.

W

WEBSITES AND INTERNET ACCESS

The most useful websites are:
www.visitlisboa.com The Welcome Centre city tourist office
www.visitportugal.com The official Portuguese tourism site

www.portugal.com Travel and tourism site
www.tap.pt TAP/Air Portugal, the national airline
www.cp.pt Comboios de Portugal, the Portuguese train network
www.pousadas.pt For the historic *pousadas*

WEIGHTS AND MEASURES
Portugal uses the metric system of weights and measures.

<h1 style="text-align:center">Y</h1>

YOUTH HOSTELS
It is best to join Hostelling International before you depart (www.hihostels. com), but you can join up on arrival. Hostels are run by and can be booked through the Portuguese Youth Hostel Association (Associação Portuguesa de Pousadas de Juventude), tel: 217-232 100; www.pousadasjuventude.pt.

They have two hostels in Lisbon: one at Rua Andrade Corvo 46 (Metro: Picoas), tel: 213-532 696; and one in the Parque das Nações at Rua de Moscavide 71 (Metro: Oriente), tel: 218-920 890.

WHERE TO STAY

Hotel prices have risen in recent years to match most Western European destinations, and at the top level they are surpassing popular cities like Barcelona. Some hotels may offer reductions in low season, though nowadays Lisbon is pretty much a year-round destination. The hotels in the Lisbon section include areas such as the Baixa, Bairro Alto, Lapa, Avenida da Liberdade, the Alfama and Belem. We've also included some suggestions out along the Estoril coast to Cascais and Guincho, north to Queluz and Sintra, and south to Sesimbra. The *pousadas* in Queluz and Palmela are well-managed chain hotels with good restaurants that occupy historic buildings.

The price indication is for a double room, with breakfast, including service and taxes in high season (April–October). In low season prices can be considerably less, and top hotels also often offer discounts for booking early at any time of year. All the hotels take major credit cards unless otherwise stated.

€€€€€	**over 200 euros**
€€€€	**150–200 euros**
€€€	**100–150 euros**
€€	**60–100 euros**
€	**below 60 euros**

LISBON

1908 Lisboa Hotel €€€€ *Largo do Intendente Pina Manique 6, tel: 218 804 000,* www.1908lisboahotel.com. This superb art nouveau hotel is the top address in fashionable Largo do Intendente. A beautifully renovated wedge-shaped flat-iron building, it has characterful and stylish rooms with balconies, the nicest overlooking the pedestrianized square. A generous breakfast is served in the classy Infame restaurant downstairs.

Albergaria Senhora do Monte €€€ *Calçada do Monte 39, tel: 218-866 002.* Perched on a hillside in Graça, a district northeast of Baixa, this simple-looking place offers good accommodation with views of the castle and the river. It has a garden courtyard, where guests can have breakfast, and a top floor bar.

Almalusa €€€€ *Praça do Município 21, tel: 212 697 440, www.almalusahotels. com.* Beautifully positioned in the corner of a historic square, this eighteenth-century building now houses a chic boutique hotel. All the rooms are different, but each includes a smart TV and digital radio, and most have period touches such as flagstone floors and fireplaces. Front rooms overlook the town hall and tram routes. There's also a downstairs restaurant and small outdoor terrace.

As Janelas Verdes €€€€ *Rua das Janelas Verdes 47, tel: 213-968 143, booking: 213 218 200; www.asjanelasverdes.com.* An elegant hotel in the sophisticated Lapa district, near the River Tagus and the Museu de Arte Antiga. This small hotel occupies the 18th-century townhouse of one of Portugal's most famous writers, Eça de Queirós, and the house next door. It has a quiet, garden-like courtyard and top-floor library. Some rooms have superb views of the river. Wheelchair access.

Hotel Avenida Palace €€€€ *Rua 1 de Dezembro 123, tel: 213-218 100, www. hotelavenidapalace.pt.* Situated right on Rossio, the major plaza in the Baixa district, the remodelled Avenida Palace is one of Lisbon's finest luxury hotels. Built in 1892, it has a magnificent, old-fashioned elegance, with sumptuous public rooms and beautiful, classically decorated accommodation. Sybarites can opt for the Louis XVI-style room. The gym offers modern fitness facilities. Wheelchair access.

Bairro Alto Hotel €€€€€ *Praça Luís de Camões 2, tel: 213-408 223, www.bairro altohotel.com.* Ultra-chic, this boutique hotel in the bohemian Bairro Alto district, in the historic heart of Lisbon, is a short walk from the main sights. Rooms are soundproofed against city noise, and have plasma TVs and upmarket styling. The terrace and café bar are relaxing places to hang out for a drink.

Hotel Borges €€ *Rua Garrett 108, tel: 210-456 400, www.hotelborges.com.* A typical old Lisbon hotel with a lot of character, the Borges has an excellent location right in the heart of the Chiado district. The rooms are spacious, and some have balconies looking over the pedestrianized street below.

Hotel Britania €€€€ *Rua Rodrigues Sampaio 17, tel: 213-155 016*, www.heritage.pt. Owned by the same family that runs other top, intimate hotels in Lisbon, the Britania, in a historic 1940s townhouse, may be the most comfortable of them all. The rooms are spacious and elegantly appointed, with marble bathrooms. The hotel, alongside Avenida da Liberdade, has been lovingly restored with genuine Art Deco touches, such as the bar. Wheelchair access.

Hotel do Chiado €€€€ *Rua Nova do Almada 114, tel: 213-256 100*, www.hoteldochiado.pt. This chic hotel occupies part of the building housing the Armazéns do Chiado shopping mall, in the heart of the Chiado district. In keeping with the upmarket surroundings, the lobby and rooms are very design-oriented, with traditional Portuguese styling. There are superb views over Alfama from the roof terrace.

Dom Pedro Palace €€€€€ *Avenida Engenheiro Duarte Pacheco 24, tel: 213-896 600*, www.dompedro.com. A swish five-star hotel, with the city's swankiest entrance, this mirrored high-rise is just north of Parque Eduardo VII and across from the Amoreiras shopping centre. Rooms, equipped with every luxury, have spectacular views of the city. Popular with American tourists and European business travellers, it has a top-flight Italian restaurant and a bistro-style café. Wheelchair access.

Four Seasons Hotel Ritz Lisboa €€€€€ *Rua Rodrigo da Fonseca 88, tel: 213-811 400*, www.fourseasons.com. One of Lisbon's oldest luxury hotels has an ugly Soviet-style exterior that could not be a greater contrast to its swanky interior, which provides the height of indulgence. Rooms with balconies offer good views over Parque Eduardo VII and busy Pombal square. Excellent restaurant, Veranda. Wheelchair access.

Heritage Avenida Liberdade €€€€ *Avda da Liberdade 28 , tel: 213 404 040*, www.heritageavliberdade.com. In a fine mansion – whose ground floor once sold herbal remedies (the counter still remains) – this hotel superbly blends tradition and contemporary style. There's a small gym/plunge pool, and the rooms come with retro fittings and great cityscapes from the top-floor rooms.

Inspira Liberdade Boutique €€€€ *Rua de Santa Marta 48, tel: 210-440 900*; www.inspirahotels.com. Near the Avenida da Liberdade, this recently renovated hotel is a designer place with admirable eco-credentials – it uses green technology, runs according to sustainable policies and supports charitable projects. Rooms are modelled around Feng Shui principles. There are two rooms for guests with disabilities.

Internacional Design Hotel €€€€€ *Rua da Betesga 3, tel: 213-240 990*, www.idesignhotel.com. This emphatically designer hotel, in a great location overlooking Rossio, Lisbon's main square, has four types of highly conceptualised, spectacular rooms – Urban, Tribe, Zen and Pop – with magazine looks and every comfort. Wheelchair access.

Jerónimos 8 €€€€€ *Rua dos Jerónimos 8, tel: 213-600 900*, www.jeronimos8.com. Go boutique in Belém at this stylish place, with sleek rooms that combine strong and neutral colours to harmonious effect. There are great views over the monastery. The Busaco Wine Bar serves rare Portuguese wines and the delicious, traditional *pastéis de Belém* custard tarts.

Lisboa Plaza €€€€ *Travessa do Salitre 7 (off Avenida Liberdade), tel: 213-218 218*, www.heritage.pt. This stylish, family-run hotel, on a quiet but convenient street, opened in the 1950s. The rooms are comfortable, and the staff helpful and friendly. The restaurant serves a generous buffet breakfast, and there's a small rooftop terrace with views over the rooftops. Wheelchair access.

Martinhal Chiado €€€€€ *Rua Flores 44, tel: 210 029 600*, www.martinhal.com. Taking up an entire block on the steep Rua Flores, this welcoming hotel is geared up to making family holidays a luxurious treat. The bright, spacious apartments have their own kitchenettes if you want to self-cater and most come with comfy bunks for kids either alongside or in a separate room from the large double beds. There's a kids' club, crèche, vaulted playroom and a fun real car to clamber into in the breakfast room. The studios make an ideal base for couples, too, who may want to eat in now and again.

Hotel Métropole €€€ *Praça do Dom Pedro V 30, tel: 213-219 030*, www.almeidahotels.pt/pt/hoteis-em-lisboa. One of Lisbon's best deals, is this classic 1920s Art Deco hotel is in the heart of the Baixa, overlooking Rossio. Rooms are generously sized and outfitted with antiques. Some rooms have castle, Baixa and Alfama views. Wheelchair access.

Olissippo Lapa Palace €€€€€ *Rua Pau da Bandeira 4, tel: 213-949 494*, www.olissippohotels.com. This lovingly detailed conversion of an old palatial mansion overlooks the River Tagus in Lapa. Opened in 1992, it remains the trendsetter in Lisbon luxury. It is surrounded by landscaped gardens, and there is an outdoor pool. Rooms are plush, with *azulejo*-decorated bathrooms; the entrance is swathed in marble and ceiling frescos. Wheelchair access.

Pensão Londres € *Rua Dom Pedro V 53, tel: 213-462 203*, www.pensaolondres.com.pt. An unpretentious *pensão* at the edge of the Bairro Alto, occupying four floors of an imposing town house just minutes away from the district's restaurants, *fado* houses, bars and clubs. There are panoramic views of the city from rooms on the 3rd and 4th floors; otherwise take in the vista from the nearby Miradouro de São Pedro de Alcântara. The rooms are small but adequately furnished, though not all have private bathrooms or toilets. Continental breakfast included.

Solar dos Mouros €€€€ *Rua Milagre de Santo António 6, tel: 218-854 940*, http://solardosmouroslisboa.com. A stylish boutique hotel up near the castle, occupies a tangerine-coloured townhouse and enjoys panoramic views over the Tagus and city. The contemporary rooms are individually designed with bold colours, African art and striking modern paintings; they also feature marble bathrooms and hardwood floors.

Hotel Tivoli Lisboa €€€€€ *Avenida da Liberdade 185, tel: 213-198 900*, www.tivolihotels.com. One of Lisbon's largest and longest-running luxury hotels, the Tivoli is right on the main thoroughfare. It excels in services and facilities, which include a noted rooftop restaurant and a heated outdoor swimming pool. Outdoor dining in summer. Wheelchair access.

VIP Executive Suites Éden €€€ *Praça dos Restauradores 24, tel: 213-216 600*, www.viphotels.com. In a famous Art Deco building right on Praça dos Restauradores, this cool, modern apartment-hotel is a great deal, especially for families. There are kitchen-equipped studios and full apartments, with daily or weekly maid service. Panoramic pool and breakfast service. Wheelchair access.

York House €€€ *Rua das Janelas Verdes 32, tel: 213-962 435*, www.yorkhouselisboa.com. Near the Museu de Arte Antiga in Lapa, several blocks west of the centre, this small, converted 17th-century Carmelite convent is in a lovely, quiet part of town. It retains the feel of a serene retreat from the outside world, and the rooms are elegant but not stuffy. There's outdoor dining in the garden courtyard during the summer and a recommended restaurant. Wheelchair access.

ESTORIL COAST

Hotel Albatroz €€€€€ *Rua Frederico Arouca 100, Cascais, tel: 214-847 380*, www.albatrozhotels.com. This mansion perched above the Praia da Rainha beach is Cascais's most elegant hotel. Public rooms and guest rooms swim in luxury, with some occupying another beautiful palace across the street. Outdoor pool and good restaurant with superb views.

Hotel Fortaleza do Guincho €€€€€ *Estrada do Guincho, Cascais, tel: 214-870 491*, www.fortalezadoguincho.com. Just outside of Cascais, in a former 16th-century fortress perched on a rocky ledge overlooking Guincho beach and the sea, this enchanting hotel is a remarkable getaway. Marvellous antique touches throughout include tile floors and period silver and crystal. Most rooms have fireplaces, and many have balconies with views of the sea – including Cabo da Roca, Europe's westernmost point.

Hotel Palácio do Estoril €€€€€ *Rua Particular, Estoril, tel: 214-648 000*, www.palacioestorilhotel.com. This 5-star luxury hotel, established in 1930, looks like a cruise ship and is as palatial as its name suggests. It has a heated outdoor pool, tennis courts and gardens, and offers guests special rates at its golf course. The top-notch restaurant serves international cuisine. Wheelchair access.

QUELUZ AND SINTRA

Pousada de Queluz, D. Maria I €€€€ *Largo do Palácio Nacional, Queluz, tel: 214-356 158*, www.pousadas.pt. Occupying the part of the royal summer palace that was formerly the domain of the Royal Guard of the Court, this pink and white *pousada* is ideal if you want to explore Lisbon and its surroundings but don't want to stay in the city. The rooms are attractive and well sized, and restaurant Cozinha Velha, across the road, which serves the delicious Marfim pudding, is one of the area's best.

Sintra Marmòris Palace €€€€€ *Avenida Barão de Almeida Santos 7, Sintra, tel: 211-146 189*, www.marmorishotels.com/en/sintra-marmoris-palace.html. Upscale hotel in a restored 19th century mansion surrounded by manicured gardens. There are nine sumptuously decorated rooms some with views of the garden and Sintra. There's also a heated outdoor pool on-site.

Tivoli Palácio de Seteais €€€€€ *Rua Barbosa do Bocage 8, Sintra, tel: 219-233 200*, www.tivolihotels.com/en/tivoli-palacio-de-seteais. A luxury hotel in a beautiful 18th-century palace, with antique furniture, manicured gardens (Lord Byron wrote here) and superb views. Some visitors find it a little dainty compared to more relaxed *quintas* nearby. Sports facilities include tennis courts, an outdoor pool and horse riding.

SOUTH OF LISBON

Hotel Club Azeitão €€ *Quinta Do Bon Pastor, Vila Fresca de Azeitão, tel: 212-198 590*, www.turim-hotels.com. This nice, old-fashion hotel is just 20 minutes from Lisbon. Amenities include a swimming pool, tennis court, business centre, restaurant and coffee shop. The green terrace is a good place to relax. Nearby is a beautiful golf course. In low season the price for a double room drops to €55.

Pousada de Palmela €€€ *Castelo de Palmela, Palmela, tel: 212-351 226*, www.pousadas.pt. A luxury *pousada* carved out of a 12th-century hilltop castle, later a headquarters of the Order of Santiago, with a quiet cloister. There are fabulous views towards Setúbal and the sea. The notable restaurant in the former refectory serves local dishes; its specialities are cod and partridge.

Sana Sesimbra Hotel €€€ *Avenida 25 de Abril, Sesimbra, tel: 212-289 000*, www.sesimbra.sanahotels.com. Modern and stylish, this hotel is just across the road from the main beach. Facilities include a restaurant and bar, and a rooftop pool with panoramic views of the bay.

INDEX

THE **MINI** ROUGH GUIDE TO
LISBON

First edition 2023

Editor: Beth Williams
Author: Matthew Hancock and Amanda Tomlin
Picture Editor: Tom Smyth
Cartography Update: Katie Bennett
Layout: Greg Madejak
Head of DTP and Pre-Press: Rebeka Davies
Head of Publishing: Sarah Clark
Photography Credits: Bigstock 24; Fotolia 67; iStock 4TL, 5T, 18, 22, 70, 71; Lydia Evans/Apa Publications 11, 13, 14, 17, 20, 26, 29, 30, 33, 34, 37, 39, 41, 42, 44, 48, 51, 53, 55, 57, 60, 63, 64, 66, 73, 74, 76, 77, 78, 79, 80, 81, 82, 84, 85, 86, 89, 91, 92, 93, 94, 96, 99, 101, 103; Public domain 4BR, 47, 59; Shutterstock 1, 4TC, 4TR, 4CR, 4CL, 4BL, 5C, 5B, 6T, 6B, 7T, 7B, 36, 69
Cover Credits: Streets of Alfama **Visual Intermezzo/Shutterstock**
Distribution
UK, Ireland and Europe: Apa Publications (UK) Ltd; sales@roughguides.com
United States and Canada: Ingram Publisher Services; ips@ingramcontent.com
Australia and New Zealand: Booktopia; retailer@booktopia.com.au
Worldwide: Apa Publications (UK) Ltd; sales@roughguides.com

Special Sales, Content Licensing and CoPublishing
Rough Guides can be purchased in bulk quantities at discounted prices. We can create special editions, personalised jackets and corporate imprints tailored to your needs. sales@roughguides.com; http://roughguides.com

Contact us
Every effort has been made to provide accurate information in this publication, but changes are inevitable. The publisher cannot be held responsible for any resulting loss, inconvenience or injury sustained by any traveller as a result of information or advice contained in the guide. We would appreciate it if readers would call our attention to any errors or outdated information, or if you feel we've left something out. Please send your comments with the subject line "Rough Guide Mini Lisbon Update" to mail@uk.roughguides.com.

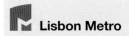

Lisbon Metro

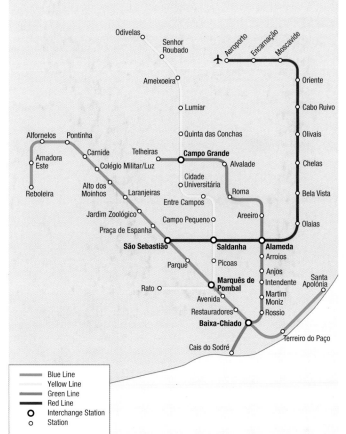

Odivelas
Senhor Roubado
Ameixoeira
Lumiar
Quinta das Conchas

Aeroporto
Encarnação
Moscavide
Oriente
Cabo Ruivo
Olivais
Chelas
Bela Vista
Olaias

Alfornelos
Pontinha
Amadora Este
Carnide
Reboleira
Colégio Militar/Luz
Alto dos Moinhos
Laranjeiras
Jardim Zoológico
Praça de Espanha

Telheiras
Campo Grande
Cidade Universitária
Alvalade
Roma
Entre Campos
Campo Pequeno
Areeiro

São Sebastião
Saldanha
Alameda

Parque
Picoas
Arroios
Anjos
Intendente
Martim Moniz
Rossio

Marquês de Pombal
Rato
Avenida
Restauradores

Santa Apolónia

Baixa-Chiado

Cais do Sodré
Terreiro do Paço

	Blue Line
	Yellow Line
	Green Line
	Red Line
O	Interchange Station
o	Station